Our American Being, Righteously Free

JIM BOWMAN

CITIOFBOOKS, INC.
3736 Eubank NE Suite A1
Albuquerque, NM 87111-3579
www.citiofbooks.com
Hotline: 1 (877) 389-2759
Fax: 1 (505) 930-7244

Ordering Information:

Quantity sales. Special discounts are available on quantity purchases by corporations, associations, and others. For details, contact the publisher at the address above.

Printed in the United States of America.

ISBN-13:   Softcover   979-8-89391-069-8

                Ebook   979-8-89391-070-4

Library of Congress Control Number: 2024907716

Table of Contents

OBAMA YEARS

PRESIDENT DONALD J. TRUMP

BIDEN

DEDICATION

This book is dedicated to all who have followed since Washington with their service and sacrifice for the preservation of our Blessed American homeland.

As always, much love and appreciation to my dearest supporter, Carol Jane.

Many thanks to Peggy Burke for her patience, friendship, and editing.

And where the Spirit of the lord is, there is liberty.

-Corinthians 3:17

FOREWORD

This book is written to stir curiosity and questioning outside of today's limited and restricted discourse. It's rooted in our American past and thus brings forth many forgotten or discarded principles which have contributed to our nation's success. Each discussion tackles many current challenges; often supported by the quotes from approximately twelve of our Founders.

The table of contents is separated into the three Presidential administrations from 2009 through 2022. While today's happenings had started to surface, this fourteen-year period also represented an incubation for today's revolutionary unrest. In defense of this anti-American lunacy, I believe that as freedom loving Americans, we all must do what we can to reverse such a dangerous venue. The issues within generally address this need. So, as you are reading these wordy delights, I'd like to express my thanks for your mutual concern that all is not right; and that America requires and always will require the protections and benefits from a proven pro American brand of leadership.

Another purpose is to spark the reader's curiosities away from one's republican, democrat or independent identities so that we all can relate to the negativity being directed against our American being. This proud identity ensures a natural obligation to preserve our heritage and traditions in order for each succeeding generation to partake in the enjoyments of freedom and to protect our American gifts.

This sense of inclusion is common to all; whether by birth or by swearing allegiance. The commonality which binds us is the theme within these pages. I might add that quite by accident, my writings number the same eighty-five which happen to be the total comprising our Founders' The Federalist Papers.

My first publishing effort, This Roar of Ours, stated that these written articles are neither of a republican nor democrat position nor are they presented with a conservative or liberal intent. My approach continues to be American only. Hopefully, within each composition, this genuine concern and love for America will not only be evident but will touch all readers.

It is understandable to ask, "Who is this Jim Bowman, never heard of him." Well, I'm not part of the crowd of authors who seem to pump out books seasonally. Hopefully, just being an average American is qualifying enough, since just like you, I've "been there and done that."

I regard my Vietnam service as an honor and in keeping pace with those fathers and husbands from my "growing up" Philadelphia neighborhood, who earned respect and love from their WWII service and sacrifice. I later married, raised a family and finally retired from the trades as a boilermaker. Along the way, as a parent, I was hard on my children, especially my daughter, who in later years thanked me but also admitted that she, at times, hated me. My reply: "Good, then I was doing my job." I might add that this type of "hard line" parenting has always worked and is sorely needed today.

A major loss within our current culture is the absence of America's traditional standards; that the policeman is our friend; that Sunday is regarded as the Sabbath and that proper attire and conduct is a classroom requirement. The elimination of such accepted societal supports directly challenges any notion of today's so-called "progress" since its negative results are impossible to ignore.

From another more practical perspective, if such a renewal takes place, approximately seventy-five percent of our income taxes should disappear! This also reveals just how far our self-feeding government has taken us from our original Constitutional dictates.

Coupled with this retro need is another missing support system; our belief and reliance upon one's chosen faith. This ageless source of support and reliance has been a natural aid to America's founding and growth. Also, in gradual fashion has been the disappearance of our individual thought processes along with common sense. Today, this has reached a point that what was seen actually wasn't! Such is today's illogical atmosphere.

Our American journey was gifted to us all at birth but as usual, anything given tends to lessen in value, especially when it's belittling is encouraged! Hopefully, this read will renew what today's version of America has chosen to cheapen and revile. Enjoy the read.

OBAMA YEARS

Enjoy Life

January 13, 2009

Just what is a worthwhile life? Is it the materialism that has hypnotized so many or are there other more basic pursuits and goals more rewarding? As a young man, these deep thoughts never surfaced but as the years pile up, one not only has the inclination but time to recount all the good and bad of one's existence.

While it may seem somewhat corny to younger readers, the essence of a fulfilling life comes down to the simplicities of health and happiness. While health was never a major thought when I was younger, it can actually take on the appearance of a personal savings account. What I mean by this is that proper youthful restraints and regimens will bear fruit in later years.

While the highly advertised addictions of alcohol, drugs and gambling easily come to mind, we all know addictions come in many shapes and sizes. I've known people that have been addicted to their careers, to the almighty dollar, to jealousy, to pornography, to winning and even to health. Anything in life that ceases to be fun by its growing compulsiveness can become detrimental.

Another point well worth realizing is that you are the captain of your ship. You hold the keys to your happiness and betterment, no one else. I remember years ago, standing on the Media Court House grounds in Pennsylvania listening to the pleasing promises of the younger candidate Bush. No more nation building topped the list of his campaign promises which were quickly forgotten.

I mention this remembrance as a lesson I learned; that only I can determine and better my future, certainly not some far removed politician who will say anything to get a vote! This self-determination is as it should be in a free society.

One almost unavoidable intrusion against an agenda for responsible conduct is the world of advertising. Its messaging is often corruptive since in many cases, it's what you want to hear. How many of us want to be told that "you need a break today?" How enticing is it when offered an "introductory no interest credit card?" Or how about leasing rather than buying a car? An offering a well-deserved vacation? These and other come-ons sound great but they all deceive their audience. And, when it's all said and done, do any of these "needs" present lasting happiness or an overall improvement to your life? All are of an immediate nature and thus lack any true or lasting value.

Ask yourself, "What is it all about?" What constitutes your happiness? What is it that you would like to be remembered for? What is of value to you? What are the lessons of life which you hold high and want to pass on to your children? Have you developed an appreciation for what is often taken for granted? Consider the first scent of spring in the air. In our fast-paced computerized world, we seem to overlook or forget what really is important. I think in many pursuits, we have lost our priority for having plain old fun.

Across the street, a younger couple, who in my estimation are more grounded than most, bought the latest computer rage called Wii for their two children. My spelling of "Wii" may be wrong since I'm not familiar with it.

However, they also bought two bikes which they stashed away with me till Christmas Eve. My point is that late Christmas day, I asked the parents how the children liked their bikes and they said they haven't ridden them as of yet since they were still playing with Wii on TV.

Now call me old fashioned, or a Neanderthal but there was a time when getting a new bike for Christmas was the ultimate! Not only that; but the parents of yesteryear wouldn't see their kids till dinner time. Sitting in front of a TV set all day, whether watching a movie or playing a game, is not as healthy as an outdoor activity. Could it be that our physical health is being sacrificed?

Another sacrifice, responsibility, has also been discarded in our race to indebtedness with ignoring such time-honored cautions as "pay as you go and you never owe." In addition, pain killers or sedatives and counseling sessions are normal supports which only increase the ease of our reckless behavior. Along the way, we have dismantled the traditional structure of the American family as we seek out the most affordable day care centers.

They say, "Life's a bitch." Well, it is what you make of it. Four elements to our existence never change. They are human nature, common sense, truth and the necessities of life. What has changed is how we acquire happiness. It used to be those "needs" were basic and useful necessities. Now, anything may be considered a "need," regardless of the price tags.

The simplicities of life are still there to be enjoyed. But it's up to you to take the time and rekindle the appreciation for what normally and what formerly would make one happy. If you can do this, your stress-filled life will disappear, and your health will improve.

Our American Indifference

March 28, 2009

On June 1, 1837, Daniel Webster remarked,

"Our destruction, should it come at all, will be from another quarter. From the inattention of the people to the concerns of their government, from their carelessness and negligence, I must confess that I do apprehend some danger. I fear that they may place too implicit a confidence in their public servants and fail properly to scrutinize their conduct; that in this way they may be made the dupes of designing men and become the instrument : s of their own undoing."

Mr. Webster's apprehensions now seem uncanny.

I think that in addition to Mr. Webster's concerns between the public's confidence and apathy, he failed to recognize the natural tendency of an emerging ignorance when all is going well.

This term "ignorance" has nothing to do with one's intelligence but rather one's lack of curiosity, interest and guarded appreciation for our Founding principles. These pre$requisites are fundamental to the preservation of freedom and liberty and as such, their depreciating regard has become the root of our dilemma, Consider John Adams' belief that, "Our Constitution was made only for a moral and religious people." Now consider our present state of higher learning from the pen of The Hartford Courant's writer Jesse Leavenworth, appearing on March 24th entitled, "Required campus reading: Wesleyan sex magazine."

Briefly outlined was the general purpose; supposedly to "bring sex into the open, to inform and express – in art, photography and prose – a topic that often dominates the college student's mind." Obviously, there's more incentive to this "refresher" course than meets the eye. Hell, this subject has been bandied about thoroughly by the time that some students even move on from grade school.

As the magazine co-editor, Yannick Bindert states, "We kind of wanted to…unlock this taboo." Being raised in Germany, Bindert joins with the European impression of Americans being sexually backward and inhibited. However, leave it to the official Wesleyan spokesman David Pesci to provide his educated piece on ignorance. To quote Wesleyan's hands off policy concerning this publication, "It comes down to freedom of speech."

Our freedom of speech is addressed in the First Amendment of the Constitution. However, this freedom is not all encompassing. By that I mean that freedom requires individual responsibility. One of those is the freedom to talk without being harmful or offensive to others. This restriction is often explained by not yelling "fire" in a crowded or confined setting.

The revisionist of our Founding principles will argue endlessly over what is to be accepted. Take for instance this expanding venue of pornography. What beneficial purpose does this "speech" provide? With similar publications at other institutions, such as Yale and Harvard, the purpose is hardly beneficial nor is it educational. During one's youthful years, the need to stimulate or heighten such urges is certainly not filling a void.

Another example of our unknowing or apathy is this ability to tax. Until 1913, our country's welfare was maintained without this federal need for taxing income. Today, taxes have reached levels of abuse which can dictate a change of a family's living standards.

Following WWII, we embarked upon the rebuilding of Europe under The Marshall Plan. Today, this has morphed into an entity known as "foreign aid," which also happens to be supported by those we elect to represent the American people! This is just one of the many unconstitutional expenditures that our "in the red" country refuses to end. Why? But more importantly, what authority was cited originally to permit this program?

Such unlawful spending doesn't stop! Currently this "bail out" era continues as Congress has already approved a $700 million package in support of Mexico's efforts to fight their drug cartels. Our new Secretary of State, Hillary Clinton, is now asking for an additional $80 million to provide for Mexico's Blackhawk helicopter purchases.

Aside to this illegitimate tax dollar spending is this increase of violence along our southern borders without any meaningful response! We enforce security at airports by harassing Americans, yet Washington remains deaf to the needs of our citizens at our southwestern border.

Citizen concerns are heard only at election time. We are not being represented and even when they do listen, they fail to act as was promised. In addition, their likely annual wage increases rile when they refuse to be responsible and represent properly.

George Washington stated,

> "Government is not reason, it is not eloquence.
> It is force. Like fire, it is a dangerous servant and
> a fearful master."

Similar to Mr. Webster's opening words of concern; both are accurate descriptions of today's Federal behemoth, which "we the people" now need to remedy!

The Reverse of Good Intention

April 18, 2009

They say that "the road to hell is paved with good intentions." This phrase, the least damning approach to our foreign follies, may describe our Nation's foreign policies since WWII.

It always amazed me that our Nation could conclude WWII with a victory in Europe, yet at the same time recognized the need to station troops there as a deterrence against Russian aggression. I mean, isn't it odd that our WWII Russian brethren suddenly became our chief Cold War adversary?

Consider where Russia would have been without America's economic and military aid when defending her homeland against German invasion. Today, we are told that Russia has shed the mask of aggression since the "Soviet Union" no longer exists. Today Russia and America are partners in trade and corporate investments! But yet, there still is a need for maintaining NATO. Our good intentions are now somewhat fuzzy.

At the conclusion of WWII, it wasn't enough that America saved Britain and the entire European continent from slavery. We then embarked upon rebuilding those devastated economies including Germany. Today, as each individual country has shed their independent sovereignty for the promised high hopes of a European Union, America is being inundated with regulatory restraints from a now unified union of "states" which our soldiers died freeing. Now, with short memories blurred by business demands and greed, America has rebuilt her "economic adversary!"

Need we rehash our folly with the rebuilding of Japan into what it is economically today? Not only have we renovated the shattered countries of our enemies, but we have also done so without any reward or repayment! Why?

In addition, America's own economic base continues to abandon her shores. Of course, not all corporations and job skills can be exported to the cheaper labor markets overseas, hence, the importation of cheap labor. Can anyone dare mutter the words, "economic treason?" Discomforting thought, yes! Far fetched, no! And this is just one treasonous entity.

While our good will sponsored our tax dollars into the European/Japanese recovery efforts, our "good intentions" embroiled us into another rescue effort to save a country, this time from the dreaded cloak of communism. Justification for intervention caused the introduction of the dreaded "domino theory." Today, not only is that formula tattered; America has economically embraced another country which was formerly our enemy. This turnaround came with a high but forgettable price.

Along with almost 60,000 lives lost, our elected representatives from both political parties chose commerce over honor and common decency. The fate of over 2000 missing Americans became secondary to the affluent behind the scenes whisperings within the Washington corridors. The shattered beliefs from such betrayal and deception continue to reverberate throughout our countryside.

From a calloused or even realistic point of view, what else was to be expected from a policy which included assassination as its opening move! American complicity concerning the assassination of Vietnamese President Diem cannot be denied. Three weeks later, another Presidential assassination took place in Dallas, Texas!

Today, we have suddenly realized the need for "globalization." Not only will this be an ECONOMIC DISASTER, BASED UPON OUR HIGHER WAGES AND LIVING STANDARDS versus the lesser economies of the world, it spells our Nation's loss of independent concerns and economic well-being. It already has tied us down with endless foreign decrees of restraints and prohibitions. In a nutshell, it accomplishes what a military action never could. It controls America through an economic noose.

With this new phase of a "world economy/community, our foes have become more imaginary. Our foreign dependence has grown as our independent industrial strength weakens. Our living standards, along with our expectations, have also drastically been lowered as our Country dives deeper into debt. Given this situation, masking our foreign mistakes under the heading of "good intentions" may just have run its course.

What remains constant through this current financial squeeze is the double talk embedded within such sacred expenditures as "foreign aid!"

I mean, what the hell is a ten trillion dollar in debt country doing giving "aid" away while it can't keep her highways repaired?

And while we are on this "what the hell" subject, just why are we in Iraq? And why the building of an "embassy" which for all intent and purposes resembles a damn city! With such an over abundant investment, who believes that by electing a new President, our Iraq chapter will come to an end? Very likely, these "good intentioned" policies have moved America closer to her own creation of hell. At least an economical one!

As a Nation, we have obviously opted for a course other than those which our Forefathers intended. As written last week, George Washington thought that "Tis our true policy to steer clear of permanent alliance with any portion of the foreign world..." He said that 213 years ago and it's more applicable today than ever before.

Over the years, consider what America has accomplished with her endless foreign involvements. The record of one "good intentioned" failure after another has not produced a single benefit. Such a record, when tallying America's sacrifice is unforgivable, if not criminal.

The April 15th "Tea Party" protests around our Country were downplayed for good reason. Americans have had it! Between oppressive taxes and a dwindling job market, the only viable employer has become the American military! This is not what our Forefathers had in mind nor is it what my generation intended for our children. Everything is shrinking except the size of the Federal Government and its addiction to spending!

Our government is in place to ensure the welfare of our country and defend and uphold the inalienable rights and freedoms of its citizens. It is now time to live and believe that "America first" is the priority when electing our leadership. God Bless America!

Who Really Drove Tiger's SUV?

January 25, 2010

After watching Peyton Manning's performance against the Baltimore Ravens and the New York Jets, I must admit that he is the NFL's number one quarterback. For as long as I can remember, the quarterback position is a football team's most important position. As such, it could be argued that Mr. Manning is the best player in the NFL.

The only other "best player" of a particular sport is Tiger Woods. However, since the PGA is not a team sport but rather an individual contest, this top designation offers good and bad aspects to the sport of golf.

Completely different from the team atmosphere, where even the best relies upon teammates for success, singling one individual as the best seems to detract from the quality and competitiveness of each player in every golf tournament. Since Tiger turned pro in 1996, he has been the favorite in all the tournaments in which he has entered.

Not only has he been the favorite, but he is also generally considered to be the best golfer, maybe of all time. With this earned adoration come all the pluses of stardom for both Tiger and his sport. Increased gates receipts, endorsements, higher advertising fees along with a renewed public interest and growth in the game itself.

Since 1996, Tiger's impact has been surreal. No other individual, with the possible exception of Babe Ruth, has had such a dynamic impact in the world of sports. Nevertheless, since his accomplishments take place within the realm of individual competition, more rides upon his success and failure than team performers. But there is also a negative possibility lurking.

As we all now know, this unwanted aspect is not about faltering on the field of play but rather, it concerns Tiger's his off the field interests and activities. Given his "squeaky clean" public image from both his charitable efforts and his popular endorsement styles, the revelations of his numerous infidelities came out of left field. The PGA is still reeling.

The current state of the PGA tour may be analogous to an investor who puts "all his eggs in one basket." The PGA rode the coattails of their headliner for years. And for years, as is the case of any "bull" market, it was quite profitable. Contrary to the diversified portfolio, which in this analogy may be represented by the diversity of team sports, the risk is higher since all success is contingent upon one player. In the early morning hours on the day following Thanksgiving, in clubhouses across the country, the good times came to a screeching halt as did Tiger's SUV.

Were there hints to this coming calamity? Maybe. As with any prima donna, allowances are expected in order to "keep the ship on an even keel." Throughout his career and TV exposure, there were instances which could be linked to the influence of "Tigermania." One infamous example came early in his professional career when a dozen onlookers moved a "moveable impediment." Prior to the next season, golf's sacred rule book corrected such an asinine interpretation concerning what was an immovable boulder.

What transpired might just be as simple as ignoring or flaunting human nature. One of our Forefather's greatest concerns, when authoring our Constitution, was the inherent threat from what they termed "the mischief of man." This was rightly attributed to our human frailties of which "greed" may lead the pack. If nothing else, greed was a major player since Tiger's emergence on the Tour. Both the PGA and Tiger were caught up in its grip. And in the end, this at least was a contributing factor.

The rules during a golf tournament are in play and strictly enforced. The rules governing "play" off the course are not so strictly scrutinized nor is the "play" itself. For such a famously wealthy and popular athlete, the differing atmosphere from the highly controlled environment of a tournament verses the more leisurely surroundings of daily living is enormous, especially for one who enjoys such "in play" considerations. This coupled with an inescapable egotism presented more than enough incentive for the type of "play" which is largely frowned upon in either setting.

As with any credible sport, the game will withstand and continue long after its headliners depart. The "Babe" has long since passed. Someday, Peyton too will hang up his cleats. Yet, both baseball and football have and will continue to grow in popularity and stature. Golf will do the same.

So it is that someday, Tiger will follow Arnold and Jack into golf's Hall of Fame since age determines competitiveness. The trick is to face that time with a bit of class. So far, that is a talent which Tiger has yet to recognize.

Thinking Not Presidential

March 7, 2010

It used to be Republican or Democrat. Then it was "conservative" or "liberal." Now, identities include "blue dog democrats" and "RINO republicans." This labeling or name calling only tends to mask and confuse while dividing and alienating Americans over any and all issues. Also, it tends to inhibit debate of current issues or between political opposites. Along the way, glamour, personalities and emotions have entered into our political thinking.

I suppose this current lessening of leadership versus stardom's appeal began with JFK. I can remember during the campaigning days of the 1960 election, voters were heard remarking, "Oh, don't they just make such a lovely couple," or "she will be such a beautiful first lady," and of course, "isn't he such a handsome man?"

What happened to leadership? While the 1960 campaign showered the voter with JFK's heroic PT109 exploits, the bottom line was glamour verses that boring Nixon.

Then Clinton became another pretty boy in our White House. Without getting into the sordid details, how could his personal "southern boy" charm and twang become equal in importance to leadership? Is it just that the youthful good looks of today's "leaders" are so preferable over the qualified candidate?

Today, personal conduct is the least of our worries, yet it is a cornerstone for leadership. As Clinton so sadly demonstrates, pretty isn't necessarily Presidential! Therefore, the needs of this candidate included an army of "spin doctors, namely our media, to discolor his history and sway future voter support.

However, his public handlers are not the issue as is the thought of the American voter even considering a candidate with such a dishonorable record when his nation called him for military service. Not only that, what does it say about our political machinery if Clinton becomes its best candidate while owning such a dishonor?

All this is now history but the unqualified continue to charm voters and win our Presidency. Today, Obama engineered an election based upon personal charm, our media's adoring treatment along with a mixture of his minority status and America's re-ignited sense of guilt.

All these elements fade into irrelevance when realizing that not only is Obama's past very murky, his proof of citizenship and "natural born citizenship," from his own words of identifying his dad as being a Kenyan citizen, disqualified his candidacy.

Again, as with Clinton, Obama's fundamental qualifications slid by the wayside versus charm, fancy oratory skills and a preferential media which renewed America's past historical sins into present day guilt.

Soon enough, the American electorate will be given a second chance in 2012 to replace and return to office a proper and qualified leader. Hopefully, these modern-day candidates' forgetfulness of their campaign rhetoric once in office, will be fulfilled with a new leader. But first, I imagine that 2012 will revisit Obama's 2008 winning formula.

The lesson to be learned is that like my dear Mother used to say, 'talk is cheap!' While pleasing to the ears, it lacks the substance or the proven worth which one's record of deeds and accomplishments presents. In Obama's case, his inspiring democratic convention speech propelled him into his party's presidential limelight. Such oratory skills negated or just blurred his limited Senate time. Again words, not deeds.

In addition to a needed upgrading by each party's presidential selections, it ultimately comes back to "we the people." When a "draft dodger" or one that fails to meet a Constitutional mandate for being our Presidency becomes elected, it is "we the people, who must reconsider our priorities and what best guarantees proper leadership. This is best addressed with a record of accomplishments, not by fancy talk or with good looks.

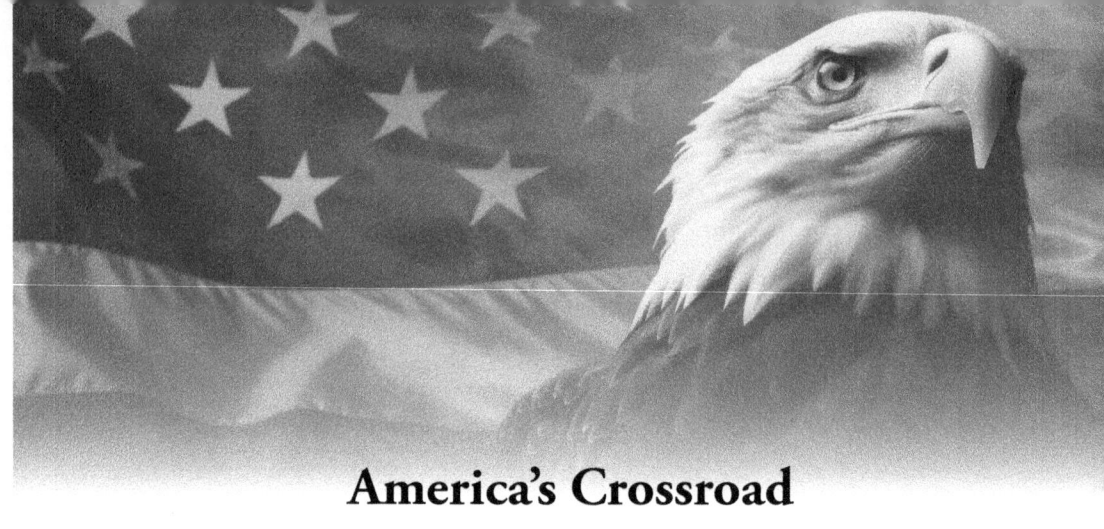

America's Crossroad

August 30, 2010

Once upon a time in my youth, an official inquisition occurred for the sole purpose of killing the messenger. This Congressional drama was quite odd in that the messenger's purpose was to ferret out any possible foreign agent who would obviously have loyalty to and would work for his or her preferred allegiance. This lengthy inquiry was the culmination after years of attempting to discourage, degrade and intimidate the messenger into ceasing his investigations.

Such a shameful event may well have provided the opening salvo which led to our current situation. From a personal point of view, while I was unaware due to my young age, I now view those early fifties debacle which as precursor which led to this fascination with socialism as there is little doubt that socialism has now claimed a foothold here in America. If current official policy is a clue, it may just be the chosen path for our future.

Of course, the McCarthy hearings are what I have pinpointed as the messenger being killed. From those questionable hearings, the one query, which has become infamous, "have you left no sense of decency, sir…" seems more relevant than ever to ask. Only this time, it is not directed to an individual but to a party and our country as a whole.

Consider that in the year which I was born, 1944, there was only one communist country in the world, Russia! I would say questions need answering but the question of America's decency tops the list.

I believe that while my life is only unique to me, it does provide the lineage to our national dilemmas. It seems that what is now taking place within the changing political landscape could be the product of years of public apathy. Along with the degradation directed at Sen. McCarthy, our national skepticism and individual guardianship were also discouraged. America's treatment of that pro-American Senator may have ricocheted a sense of intimidation down to the average citizen. Today, our sleep may well be ending, and it probably took the most radical of Presidential Administrations to arouse us from our deep slumber.

Deep down inside, as time and experience grew, the basic "whys" and "hows" formed one unanswerable query. From the late seventies, my challenge became, "Is there anything that would unite America into action?" Sadly, this still awaits a firm answer.

As a Vietnam veteran I read about our immediate declaration of war following the sneak attack on Pearl Harbor. I often wondered about Korea? How did we "go to war" without a Congressional declaration? Back during Vietnam, I also wondered the same. Three thousand died at Pearl while we lost over fifty-six thousand in Vietnam without any official declaration!

The final chapter of this treason that is Washington's was the "peace with honor" accord which officially ended the hostilities against the forces of South Vietnam. I say treason since within those Kissinger pages, it was understood that if the forces of North Vietnam ever attempted to invade the South, America would once again come to its defense. The invasion took place while America turned her head.

Looking back on "my war," the lack of a declaration provided the atmosphere for what took place on campuses across our nation. I have come to the conclusion that this was by design. It may well have been for encouraging the further establishment of this socialistic rhyme. All this with a governmental nod since a declaration would have brought a legal and thus an immediate cessation of all protest.

Following Vietnam, America continued to push the odds in that it produced a near perfect record of defeats, quagmires and murky or miscued foreign entanglements. Think about it, since that time, communism has flourished within our own borders. Unbelievably, our former enemies, the ones that we were determined to stop from spreading their communist dogma around the world, those guys are now our "global" trading partners.

Change could be on the way. Across our beautiful landscape, people are arising from their intermittent siestas. A sense of Americanism and a return to our constitutional cornerstone is becoming more and more evident. This along with the notion that these questionable policies and our public's apathy has finally run its course.

This time of need may be close to the unique groundbreaking by our Forefathers. This perception of a party, which in fact is not an official political party, may well be as groundbreaking today as was Thomas Jefferson's beliefs that "rights were inherited at birth from our Creator," not from government! How to attack a party which is without official status? How to detract what comes from the heart? How to slow down, let alone reverse, this honesty, this truth and this overall sense of urgency? Truth is one heck of an adversary. Our Forefathers remained truthful to their words, actions and deeds. They swore their effort with their "lives, fortunes and sacred honor." Who among us would dare equal such devotion?

In opposition stand the deceitful, the manipulative, the power hungry and the usurpers foaming with their anti-American agenda. Their schemes and tactics are without limitations. As these dire times demand, their attempts will become more extreme and with each successive ploy, they will reveal more of their corruptive tendencies and tactics. Already, a heightened attempt to temper the Tea Party growth is from their old reliable race card, as media pundits bellow that Tea Party gatherings include racial overtones.

Knowledge is power. Combine that knowledge with comparisons and the Tea Party will become even more understandable and justified. Compare then versus now. Back then, there was the least amount of taxes and regulations with the highest amount of freedom and opportunity. Today, taxes and regulations abound with dwindling amounts of freedom.

This comparison both illustrates the inherent reasoning behind our Tea Party's formation while also revealing the degree to which our Country has been steered away from her original design. As such, the fact that America is worthy of protecting and saving makes "Tea" the choice for both our united actions and as our symbolic beverage.

In Support of Our American Heritage

July 2, 2011

Much has taken place over the month of June and as expected, Obama has continued to reveal more and more of his insolent Marxist agenda. Few can now argue that he is on a mission to destroy America as we know her. Our path is as clear as our determination is fixed.

What has taken shape is the validation that our Country is under attack from within. I don't mean just a difference of political opinions or priorities. No! This is about two camps of thought. One a Constitutional America while the other, a globalized Marxist crematorium!

No longer can we just sigh or walk away from what we are facing. Our way of life and our very freedoms are at stake. These minions of Trotsky and Leninist policies are now showing their hands in a most arrogant and threatening manner. They believe, as validated by their "in your face" actions, that they have the numbers to carry their quest to victory. For you see, numbers are what it's all about. It's what public education is all about! In addition, they also hedge their bets upon owning the White House! That's their ace! If all else fails, there's always the abused "executive order" route.

Do not misunderstand this exception. Throwing the bum out in '12 will not fold their tents. It's just that with Obama in place, they have a puppet that shortens the necessary steps for achieving their goals. So, these next sixteen months will be as critical as they may be frustrating. However, perspective is everything. These months will entail the best our enemy has to offer. November will be our election tsunami!

As our struggle continues, certain hidden elements have surfaced and through their appearance, contribute to this vista of anti-Americanism which we have unknowingly nurtured. One such entity was reported in surprising fashion in a US News and World Report item. For me personally, it tied up, explained, and validated many loose ends and personal suspicions. I am amazed that this revelation took place, but it just bolsters the position that our opposition smugly relies upon their assumption of superior numbers. This will be proven to be a tactical error and one of monstrous proportions since its anti-American nature encapsulates and identifies the enormity from their threat.

Before detailing this surprising gift, let me just quickly mention that again, while the majority of Americans supported Sen. Joe McCarthy's righteous investigations of the fifties, Washington's bi-partisan betrayal of his efforts have largely energized the "assassins" who now seem confident of administering our possible destruction.

What follows are excerpts from the above-mentioned US News and World Report It seems that according to a Harvard University study which was recently and inexplicably released, "Fourth of July celebrations in the United States shape the nation's political landscape by forming beliefs and increasing participation, primarily in favor of the Republican Party."

Harvard Kennedy School Assistant Professor David Yanagizawa-Drott and Bocconi University Assistant Professor Andreas Medestam wrote, "Fourth of July celebrations in Republican dominated counties may thus be more politically biased events that socializes children into Republicans." Also, "There is no evidence of an increased likelihood of identifying as a democrat, indicating that Fourth of July shifts preferences to the right rather than increasing political polarization." And finally, "Surprisingly, the estimates show that the impact on political preferences is permanent, with no evidence of the effects depreciating as individuals become older."

This offers an entire wide screen vista of understanding to so many previously unanswered questions. It also demonstrates the nature of instruction which is saturating the minds of our young. Is there any wonder as to why and how there is such a growing anger and feeling of guilt for being a citizen of such a successful and prosperous nation? As mentioned in other issues, Sen. McCarthy's hearing sent the fear of whatever (it wasn't 'God' since communists do not believe in religion or any "God") into the horde of governmental turncoats and thus many who took root in our colleges and universities.

Harvard, being the most prestigious and the most expensive of these institutions, somehow bolsters such beliefs. Along with assimilating into this anti-American brand of thought, our egotistical and pampered "children," eventually graduate and strengthen the ranks of American discord as they matriculate into positions of authority and leadership, many within the corporate sector; all because their parents had the wallets to subjugate their children into this socialistic doctrine for the sake of possessing a most influential door-opening degree. We, on the other hand, being appreciative and proud Americans, realize that the monetary sacrifice was nil versus the mental indoctrination which their sons and daughters endured.

There's more to this bit of information. This report supplies evidence as to why the crowd numbers are so meager, not just at Independence Day celebrations but at all similar patriotic occasions.

It has been a common assumption that Memorial Day and Veterans Day parades only brought out veterans and their families. This was the excuse given as to why so many refrained from participating. While some basis of truth probably exists, based upon past rebellious actions, it now appears that there is more to this absence than meets the eye. As such, there is a need to reverse this trend. Never before was there more reason to attend a patriotic ceremony or parade and wave our American flags.

We have an obligation to our Country and to the children which we lovingly raise. We have the duty to reverse what these insidious plotters are so intent upon enacting over us. And do not think that turning out for an Independence Day parade is trite or ineffectual. Everything we do must be in their face, as are their daily insults to us. We must tend to our children so that they grow into proud Americans. We must not only take the time but in many cases "make the time" to reacquaint ourselves with what we often took for granted, our American inheritance!

Consider what this Harvard report is all about. They actually see the need to alert their fellow brethren, to protect their offspring from the disease of Americanism. If Harvard sets the tone, which it does as our Nation's most acclaimed university, do not minimize the snowball effect filtering down through academia. And this is not just limited to our prestigious campuses. These current cadres of public-school teachers were similarly indoctrinated and are instituting this anti-American dogma within their classrooms; this, due in equal parts from curriculum furnished from our federal government and from what they themselves have willingly consumed.

In the end, this Harvard report, from an American institution almost as old as America itself, targets the very essence of Americanism. I mean, we are not talking about trivia, the subject happens to be the very essence of our glorious beginning, the day in which we proclaimed our independence from an abusive authority.

July Fourth is our American heritage, our roots. This is THE American holiday of liberty and freedom! This scared day must return to the meaning which our Forefathers rallied around. This also must be our rallying point.

On our Independence Day, a few words from our gallant Forefathers: John Jay wrote,

> "My affections are deeply rooted in America…I can never become so far a citizen of the world as to view every part of it with equal regard."

And from John Adams,

> "Posterity! You will never know how much it costs the present generation to preserve your freedom! I hope you will make good use of it! If you do not, I shall repent it in heaven that I ever took half the pains to preserve it!"

Our Forefather's sacrifice, starting with their pledge to each other of their lives, fortunes and sacred honor are obviously ignored on the Harvard campus. This was not the intention when establishing the Christian based institutions of Harvard, Yale, Princeton and others. Of course, the same thing can be said for our federal government.

This particular July Fourth should be our day of re-dedication. In sad retrospect, all this could not happen if it weren't for an inattentive populace. We all share the blame. As the Tea Party now demonstrates, the time for accusing and finger pointing is past. Electing a Constitutional

President is our Delaware River crossing. RINOs and democrats need to be placed on the endangered species list.

Maybe instead of wishing "Have a happy 4th," it should be what it is, "Have a happy Independence Day." It's worth it just to identify those with quizzical stares! God Bless America!

An Infected Judiciary

September 30, 2011

As each verdict is aired, they are now appearing as a judiciary version of making a mountain out of a mole hill. If it was only that simple! I mean really, just what is legal anymore? How can one District Court find Obama's Health Care legal while another finds parts illegal and another rules that the entire Health bill is unconstitutional? Is this what a "living Constitution" is all about?

On January 31, 2011, Florida Federal Judge Vinson declared that "The Patient Protection and Affordable Care Act" to be unconstitutional. Within his conclusion, Judge Vinson wrote, "Because the individual mandate is unconstitutional and not severable, the entire Act must be declared void."

From Judge Vinson's seventy-eight-page summary judgment, my excerpt, while brief, conveys the heart of the Judge's ruling. Again, with this iron clad conclusion, how can other black robes disagree and still maintain the mantle of constitutionality?

The vast majority of Americans have fought tooth and nail against this Health Care violation of our individual liberties. When public opinion generates such a strong resentment against a particular judicial finding, then it's usually the ugly head of judicial activism which drives this rebuke. As such, with each judicial contradiction, our former granite reliance and belief in the rule of law diminishes.

Much of what our legal system pivots around today comes from past interpretations were themselves based upon interpretations. In fact, current Law School standards abide by curriculums based not upon any Constitutional tenets but upon former Supreme Court decisions. It stands to reason that such a hand-me-down system can often become untethered from the law's strict and needful adherence.

Consider the era when our Forefather's wrote our Constitution. Over time, word definitions have undergone much change. During this past year, I became familiar with Noah Webster's 1828 premier American Dictionary. Even its format was different in that modern versions follow each word with a pronunciation or syllable breakdown. Not so in Webster's first presentation. Also, Webster's definitions often contained connotations which referenced Christianity! Obviously and sadly, this has given way to this modern-day influx of secular perspectives.

The difference between then and now is so dramatic that when confronted with comparison, one must wonder about the reasons for such change and the extent of its totality. As such, how can current study of American law be so enamored with definitions and modern-day interpretations which lacked relevance to the original meanings of the law when written? This seems like the workings of a lawless judiciary!

And to this mix of changing definitions and latitudes of interpretations is the art of improvisation. The infamous Supreme Court Everson v. Board of Education ruling presented the first reference to "the wall of separation between Church and State." Today, this legally irrelevant phrase reverberates as if being the Constitutional bedrock of our religious restraints. In reality, that Everson finding simply borrowed a written phrase from a private Thomas Jefferson letter! Talk about improvising!

What's necessary to understand is that while our Supreme Court may rule upon Health Care's illegitimacy, our Judicial Branch is not authorized to legislate. Somewhere along our journey, we were led to believe that decisions from our highest court constituted "the law of the land." Even though this blends into the Court's penchant for redefining, re-interpreting and improvising, the Court's authority is strictly limited to ruling on individual cases, not to making law! No further questions, case closed!

Our Challenge

December 9, 2011

What is taking place in America today is another phase of a systematic and well-coordinated attempt at accomplishing what a force of arms could never envision. Think about it. The results from being conquered through military conquest impart negativity with a resoluteness to eventually retake what was forcefully taken away. Military gains are thus limited. However, the ability and effort to convert loyalties, beliefs and average thinking are more lasting. Today, the only question is when to accelerate the change for its final thrust for control!

During my lengthy lifetime, the object has always been the American mind. During the last half of the twentieth century till today, our citizens have been inundated with questionable if not outright anti-American nonsense. As a result, today we have a sizable portion of our people who do not know their country or her glorious history. This is a result of an attempt to weaken our resolve and to slowly introduce contradictory concepts and beliefs against our Declaration of Independence, our Constitution, our Bill of Rights and our way of life. The terms "internationalism" and "globalism" only soft peddle the harshness from the reality of what awaits.

Our journey from Bunker Hill and Valley Forge to the present has been glorious but at the same time disgracefully obvious, if viewed by one given perspective. Consequently, we now have a President who claims that our system of free enterprise and capitalism "doesn't work, it has never worked." Sadly, those listening to Obama's latest spewing in Osawatomie Kansas cheered!

Communism takes hold in poor countries. If America is to be coerced into communism, economic changes are necessary. Approximately thirty years ago, what began as "downsizing the corporate fat" grew into relocating to more friendly tax States. This gave way to foreign locations offering cheaper labor. Very telling is that all of this is without Washington 's protective attempt to modify or reduce corporate tax rates so as to create a more friendly business climate here at home.

Now, couple this exodus with the increasing amount of educational mush being dispersed into each successive generation. The results of both venues must be a shrinking economy along with a growing degree of public ignorance.

What to do? Our government's only effort was to increase all forms of benefits. How effective or practical is this? Its solution? Forget the corporate flight; just increase the ease of unemployment! In addition, we have a President who condemns the successful and the wealthy!

Then with this President's call for increased taxation, his position will only dampen rather than stimulate businesses. Overall, the government has become the culprit, yet our financial center of Wall Street bears the brunt of its misdeeds from the misdirected chants of our younger citizens. As is the case, government only takes; from business and its employees alike, it's not designed to produce. It only survives off the labor of its citizens!

America is special because of Her Blessings of freedom. This is hard to erase from both one's memory and one's heart. Just maybe these greedy opportunistic communists have impatiently jumped their gun. There's an election looming with Americans still owning their right to vote. It's people's chance to speak and they will!

Out of Control

December 17, 2011

"'Tis the season to be merry." However, the days are dwindling for the average American to still claim freedom as his ability to buy a necessary, practical and efficient household item, owning over a century length durability, the one-hundred-watt incandescent light bulb, is now limited since this time-tested product will become illegal staring on January 1, 2012.

To begin with, our response of "are you kiddin' me" just doesn't quite do it justice, as is similar to its extinction. How many Americans can relate to watching government flubbing one policy after another? In concurrence, this is a policy which defies common sense, given its lengthy usefulness. Just how much interference from authority can we tolerate before the boot on our throat becomes insufferable?

The 2007 democrat Congress passed the Energy Security and Independence Act of which President Bush then signed into law. The title's words "Security" and "independence" are insulting nonsense. How does outlawing such a reliable product ensure either term? If anything, our independence of selection has been stifled. Americans are being forced into buying a curly bulb which ominously is made in China. This absurdity finds government forcing the closing of our manufacturing centers so that we can support China's manufacturing. So much for "security" or "independence!"

This so-called Act is an act of betrayal! It was bandied about Congress that this insanity would be shelved, starting with a pro-American vote in both Houses. Our illustrious Senate never got the word since that same Senate cited the eradication of the incandescent age would, in turn, reduce the need for new power plants. This absurdity, to base rationalizing on a one-hundred-watt bulb to the stage eliminating the need for "twenty-four coal-type electric plants" defies any system for equational understanding.

Subsequent reasoning which led to this particular legislation being passed cited inefficiency and wasted energy. Such was the flimsy excuse for such a negative action against one of the most standard and reliable products ever made!

It's interesting to note that while we all rage against the evil Washington lobbyists; we at the same time ignore its most effective branch. That would be the environmentalist greasing of the Washington corridors. Now awaiting the outcome from this influence is the Presidential action concerning the Keystone pipeline project from Canada to Texas. Our President, as was likely the case with former President Bush, will be swayed not to endorse an instant 20,000 plus jobs project based upon the concerns and goals from this radically led environmental fringe.

In typical gradualist fashion, today it's the one-hundred-watt bulb, next year it will be the seventy-five-watt followed by the sixty and forty-watt bulbs in 2014.

In conclusion, talks still are heard of dispersing of those Americans who followed the communist dogma into these environmental enclaves. Judging from their lobbying results, their influence seems frightening as they apparently have the power to eliminate common sense from the equation. This scenario feeds the complacency of an American "go along to get along" approach. This is so out of control, what's next, raising that monstrous red flag?

Why Diversify America

December 24, 2011

While America's normal Christmas season observances now ignite the antics of the anti-Christians and their wannabes, it nevertheless brings home the message that nothing is off-limits or insignificant. It has become painfully clear that our country, along with Her heritage and traditions are in the cross hairs of an out-of-nowhere "diversity" revolt.

The very word "diversity" introduces an antithetical approach to our American unity and our American way of life. The definition of this word "diverse" is, "different from one another." This is as simple and anti-American as it gets! How is it that after two hundred plus years of united American States that this diversity scheme is now a required societal need? Being so diametrically opposed to our founding tenets, what could justify this reversal?

Reactions to our "Merry Christmas" greetings come with a youth-based attitude of resentment which no doubt has been fed to our young. Our openness, warmth, friendliness and well wishes from this seasonal greeting reflect upon a religious America's inherent cohesiveness. Sadly, this negative retort from our youth bears directly upon their schooling influence.

Results from this instruction are noticeably becoming varied and numerous in our society. This is a result from an educational product's adoption of a curriculum which is directly confrontational to America's Founding and purpose. Such a negative Christmas attitude also calls into question our basic Christian heritage.

Consider the turn around America has undergone from what was to what is now being accepted. Almost overnight, those who caused major losses of American life have become, supposedly, our peaceful trading partners. Also revealing its ageless allure, "the buck" has erased our communist angst! Also forgotten or forgiven is communism's "Godless" creed, which ironically lines up with this current season of rebuke.

The comfort zones of modern America have introduced a sort of idleness throughout much of our land. Hard choices or difficult predicaments are now shunned or avoided as are perceived insults or threats. The assumption is that all will clear up in the morning. These un-American attitudes and vulnerability invite only the mischief which has unfolded.

Our "Merry Christmas" greeting is but one example of our disregard. Another is this emerging foreign mindset, which finds assimilation so pleasing and necessary. For instance, our Federal Justice Department rejected South Carolina's law requiring voters to show photo identification at the polls. Assistant Attorney General Thomas Perez stated that thousands of minorities might not be able to vote because they lack the designated identification.

Our objections now pit Republicans, who enacted this photo ID law, against the Democrats who apparently care more about the vote numbers than about election integrity. This situation highlights the negativity from this hovering air of "diversity." Not only has this all-inclusive mindset shredded our societal cohesiveness and traditions, but it also now questions our common-sense legal standards which previously were accepted and non-political.

This ongoing transformation of our American being is intentional! It has to be when based upon its consistency without any let up. As our festive Christmas season validates, their attack mode is from all quarters. Amid this do-or-die period, I am reminded of a great Statesman who warned of this 'in house' communist peril long ago.

In defense of this growing presence, Americans were informed that the late Senator McCarthy's actions were not of a patriot but rather that of a drunken lout who bullied the defenseless. When remembering that this current communist infiltration was what Senator McCarthy attempted to uncover, our Christmas season would still be traditionally greeted and welcomed had America only listened. Merry Christmas to all!

A Return to Simplicity

February 14, 2012

The days of limited or simplistic governing are long gone. Authority always tends to grow, despite all the checks and balances which our Forefathers had the foresight of instituting.

Today, Washington resembles the back-and-forth bounces of a tennis match. On one side of the net stands our limited constitutional authority while the other offers the gargantuan intricacies of limitless authority and unrestrained spending. In its shorter version, the net separates legality from illegality. In this match, futility and despair very often become the onlookers.

Amid all this confusion and interwoven dependency, a distant light beckons with sanity and simplicity. We must slow down, amid our hustle and bustle, to notice that it shines on a simpler time when the slowness of a horse and buggy ride also brought time to appreciate all of God's many gifts.

Our Forefathers, with their creation, was but one example of what modern society either dismisses or has little time to appreciate. We need to step back, slow down and breathe in the air of days past, when in that era, common sense ruled, and everyday rudiments mattered. A sampling of that may well provide our sense of being and correct our course.

Those who studied our Founding Era are familiar with the names of Washington, Jefferson, Monroe, Franklin and Adams. However, that period abounds with lesser known but equally gifted Forefathers who contributed greatly to the creation of our Constitutional Republic.

One such individual was a man uniquely named St. George Tucker. He was an active participant and leader in our Revolution and bore great influence upon our Nation's system of laws.

Born in St. George, Bermuda, hence the probable source of his name, he arrived in Virginia in 1771. He rose to the rank of Colonel during the war and distinguished himself at the Battle of Guilford Court House. As a colonel of cavalry, he received wounds at the Siege of Yorktown. I mention his military record with respect to his recent Virginia arrival and of his eagerness to fight and sacrifice for our independence after such a brief period in America.

In 1796, Tucker wrote an essay and addressed the Virginia assembly regarding the abolition of slavery. In it, he noted this was of "great importance for the moral character of the citizens of Virginia." Amazing what "education" omits these days.

St. George Tucker authored, A View of the Constitution of the United States, which was published in 1803 and was considered as the premier handbook of lawyers, judges and statesmen for well over fifty years. It was the first detailed accounting and commentary of the Constitution following its ratification on September 13, 1788.

As was the prevailing sentiment of that time, Tucker was a chief proponent of state rights and limited government. Similar with today's apparent dislodge within the Republican ranks, namely the newly arrived Tea Party versus the older and more established RINO elements, Tucker's era envisioned republicans either as associated with his "Jeffersonian" branch or its northern counterpart of "commercial" republicanism. So, as one can readily see, special interests were alive and well way back then.

A side note, back in the day, special interests were commonly referred to as factions and none other than George Washington warned "against the baneful effects of the Spirit of Party." I might add that these concerns, again similar with today, reflect upon our Forefather's acknowledgments and attempts to curtail the frailties of human nature as they structured their system of checks and balances within our constitution. For this reason and contrary to modern day revisionism, our constitution remains as relevant as when it was first written.

An applicable quote found on page 16 of Mr. Tucker's highly regarded Constitutional volume offers useful insight for today's burdensome and unauthorized government.

His lengthy assessment is worthy of study. To quote:

"If an acquaintance with the constitution and laws of our country be requisite to preserve the Blessings of freedom to the people, it necessarily follows that those who are to frame laws or administer government should possess a thorough knowledge of these subjects. For what could be more absurd than that a person wholly ignorant of the constitution should presume to make laws pursuant thereto? or that one who neither understands the constitution nor the law, should boldly adventure to administer the government! Yet such instances occur not infrequently in all countries, and the danger that they will frequently occur in this, is perhaps greater than in any other."

I might add that punctuation and spelling are exact from Mr. Tucker's time.

His message, that it is absolutely necessary to promote and elect people with impeccable standards, stands as a testament as to what is currently amiss at all levels of government. We need dedicated, honest and knowledgeable individuals who place our country over the whims of its many factions and self-interest.

The governmental operations during the many decades following our Founding remained quite small and efficient. This in itself is an unmistakable message; couple that with today's reality—the mammoth governmental growth of illegal departments, bureaucracies and regulations.

The simplicity of one and one is two is easily transferred to the equation of legal produces prosperity and opportunity versus illegal produces debt and dependency. Again, our solution is quite simple. Government is not brain surgery! It's solely for the maintenance and defense of our country, the protection of our citizens, their freedoms and property.

In accordance with the words of St. George Tucker, today's general lack of foundational understanding spells disaster. How many Representatives, Senators and even Presidents are familiar with the limitations of our Constitution and also abide by the original intentions of our Forefathers? I seem to remember the Speaker of the House being asked if the new Health Care legislation was Constitutional. Her answer, "Are you crazy, are you crazy" still resonates. She later insultingly responded, and I'm paraphrasing, we have to pass the legislation to know what's in it!

St. George Tucker wrote of this exact problem over two hundred years ago. There are many in government who will never study or abide by our Constitution. This is a problem! But come November, it will be "we the people" who should be Constitutionally aware! Folks, it's simplicity that provides our way back and it is as simple as one plus one equals two!

America's White Hat

March 13, 2012

My generation grew up without any thought to criminal forensics. We were only regaled by tales of taming the West and of the heroes who won WWII. The cowboys were the good guys, and the Indians were the bad guys. It was a white-hat-verses-a-black hat thing.

Although categorized as entertainment, it was both wholesome and historically linked. And most importantly, it promoted Americanism. Each generation grew up proud and ready to defend against any foe. This recall of mine reflects back on an America that needs to return. We need to put our white hats back on.

It is often said that "kids today know so much more than we did at their age." Often, this is posed as a good thing. Well, how about if it is a bad thing? I for one do not want to send my grade school child off to study about alternate lifestyles or about the "grown-up" concerns which continue to confound the parents of today.

And speaking of parents, where are they? If I remember correctly, it was back in the seventies when unproven theories were automatically adopted. Who remembers the transformational bombshell which praised divorce? It was suggested that children would benefit since their surroundings would not be of such a rancorous setting. Few mentioned that such rancor often set the tone for what life may be offering in later years.

In addition to what would become an accepted yet costly mode for removing these argumentative and/or dysfunctional family venues, women of the day were also alerted to the fact that they should be individually challenged and gain self-worth, as in "be all you can be." There was an "old boy's network" and a hypothetical "glass ceiling" which needed breaking.

Then, the final lure affecting the family structure came from the world of economics. Voila, the introduction of the term "dual incomes." It was theorized once again that "in today's world, one income just can't make ends meet." Besides, the lady of the house was being held back from breaking through that glass ceiling, so in order to take that "needed vacation that you deserve," a solution would be another income.

I cite these monumental changes from this "new age" approach as a useful reflection to the "change" which today, has affected our society. Fully realizing that political careers pivot on the promise of change, hasn't America experienced her fair share already? Rather than change, I think time has come to at least step off the escalator and start walking backward to what worked. The prodding and pushing which our people have endured, must be recognized for what it is and what it has sadly abolished.

This transformation was choreographed. It had to be, when judging the timing and magnitude of it all. Put to rest any thought from innocent happenstance. If and when our people recognize our need and worth for a return to common sense decision making, unemotionally clear thought for returning to our traditional foundations, this perspective will bear the seed of truth and the fruit of success.

Already, the resistance to this turnaround can be observed through Santorum's uphill struggle. It's a struggle against many foes. In addition to the obvious challenge of Romney and eventually Obama, his support is siphoned by the stubborn presence of two former contenders. I term both "former" since at this point; Gingrich and Paul have become Romney's greatest assets. If their claims of remaining through the convention are held, they may eventually provide assistance to Obama's re-election. Their interfering presence is troublesome.

This subject of a traditional America and our need for its return is all about the Santorum campaign. Likewise, it has generated a stiff resolve against not only Santorum's candidacy but also his message of God, family, country. This fevered pitch has reached such a crescendo, that in a hypothetical three-man race, having to choose Romney, Obama or Santorum, Rick would be the Republican Establishment's third choice!

This third-place finish is logical given that Santorum's appeal is perceived as a severe threat to their hidden agenda. Any thought to former traditional values, a la Santorum, is perceived as the Establishment's death sentence.

Consider the preceding points from our changing American landscape. The overall or number one target from all this revamping has been our traditional values. It's as simple as when a ship flounders without its rudder. since America's rudder has always been our traditions of God, family, country.

The correlation between Santorum and the truthful beliefs of Tea Party members spells doom to the Republican hierarchy. Listen to their talking heads, its pontificators if you will. The elders of this supposed conservative party are voicing their anti-Santorum venom at will. The midterm elections were a bitter pill. This Republican shadow is determined to end this current inner party uprising here and now. Scuttling Santorum's campaign represents their preservation.

It is correct when viewing this election in terms of America's continuation as a free and independent Country or as one that will become enslaved as is Europe's lot. The hideousness of Obama's health care nightmare introduces a restriction against personal freedom and individual choice as it will pave a one-way street towards socialism.

The path on which our society has traveled in the last fifty years is not accidental. Neither are the intentions from a nucleus of socialist minded Americans who sadly have attained leadership positions. America needs the guidance of a traditional leader and Santorum wears that white hat proudly.

The Battle is Waging

May 14, 2012

In 1789, John Adams stated that, "Our Constitution was made only for a moral and religious people. It is wholly inadequate to the government of any other." These words of caution provide a reflective focus back versus the present while portraying just how far away we have drifted from America's original design. Without the set limitations erected by our Founding Fathers, the freedom which they sacrificed to obtain becomes a destructive weapon leading to our demise.

Freedom, at its most elementary level, requires limitations and responsibility. I mean, how may freedom be enjoyed if unrestrained? In that context, who is without possible harm? So no, freedom demands its own shoreline, its own useful precautions. It must, since the freedom to act within a society works hand in hand with its required dos and don'ts. Today, what we are experiencing is the elimination of those societal barriers and along with it, our willing acquiesce to unbounded freedoms. Either black or white, both are turning into grayness.

In support of freedom, through its limiting influences, is our waning religious devotion and attendance. Check on any given Sunday either from participation or observing those leaving their particular place of worship. The age discrepancy is obvious. Only a fool would not agree that our houses for worship are on borrowed time. And as John Adams warned, without a "moral and religious people," our government is inadequate.

What is taking place is intentional and reeks of a conspiratorial design. The demographics of religious worshippers provide conclusive proof that for the last fifty or so years, weekend services have experienced a series of soft ridicule and social innuendos of doubt. This is in addition to the economic strains placed upon the modern family unit and the secular adjunct offered through our tax-funded public educational system. The results from these and lesser social influences have combined to weaken our societal structure, and particularly our religious moorings.

Contrary to the army of high-browed revisionists, our country was and remains based upon a basic Judeo/Christian heritage. The Constitution's

accompanying "freedom of religion" has now been prostituted to a point, especially at the public educational level, that America would have floundered if not for the influence from a multitude of other beliefs; which if truth be known, gained their foothold of worship as a follow up to our Constitutional independence.

My brief accounting provides the background to the latest example which illuminates an organized effort to weaken our religious and moral resolve. As such, this must be recognized for exactly what it represents. We are under attack from the sinister forces of communism, pure and simple. Since WWII, our history has been replete with embarrassing setbacks and outright failures when combating this evil dogma. Why would it cease to exist now?

As writer Mark Levin in part points out in his latest work, Ameritopia, "Communism abolishes all eternal truths; it abolishes all religion and all morality…" So, why this continuing ridicule of our religious beliefs if not in conjunction with a Marxist agenda? And what to make of our dalliance with a President who refuses to acknowledge American exceptionalism?

In a May 13th Michael Gerson editorial entitled, A Generational Shift, the writer obviously applauds Obama's support of gay marriages through his boasting of rising statistics depicting a "nonreligious preference" from the 18–29-year-olds. He also cites similar statistical rises in that same age category with regards to support for gay marriages and "premarital sex as 'never wrong.'"

Gerson's essay identifies this age group as "the millennial generation" and states that "The baseline for social liberalism is starting higher than in previous generations…" He suggests that this millennial generational influence "will influence the way conservatives argue" to a point that positions voiced in the Republican primary "will not be an option." He concludes that "the impact of a generational shift in cultural attitudes is only the beginning."

This bit of anti-American written prattle is antithetical to our Judeo/Christian heritage and thus provides evidence as to the brazen type of challenge which God fearing and hardworking Americans are now contending against. And as the numbers show, the target is the young and impressionable.

What our young lack is the yardstick of comparison. Their minds are similar to rudderless ships being tossed around on a stormy sea. As such, statistics reveal that those anti-American forces, those bent upon bringing in a one world communist rule believe that they have time on their side.

However, in an ironic twist, the hand of our adversaries has been played prematurely by an interloper who only listens to his revenge filled heart as his beliefs are driven by his father's hatred. For this, the contest has commenced a wee bit early in that many remain from another American era when decency, morality, authority and restraint were in vogue.

These qualities have been revived through our Tea Party unity. I would be remised if my glee wasn't mentioned as to the recent Lugar comeuppance. Prior to that Indiana Republican primary, our liberal/socialist media, which includes Gerson, sang the praises and hoped that what happened in 2010 was just a hiccup on their road to American dominance. Now, Indiana has spoken, as will a Wisconsin governor.

I mention these isolated dramas so that the total picture can be presented. We are beset by an all or nothing contest and a no holds barred campaign season. We will need all we can muster in the face of a political party which prefers the dark side. It thus behooves us to ask our Almighty for his support and guidance.

There is a reason why this anti-American element is intent upon snuffing out our religious beliefs and reliance. As insufferable as Gerson's article was, he frames the object, an object which was and is succinctly defined in the words of President George Washington.

That gallant General and President, wrote in a March 11, 1792, letter:

> "I am sure that never was a people, who had more reason to acknowledge a Devine interposition in their affairs, than those of the United States; and I should be pained to believe that they have forgotten that agency, which was so often manifested during our Revolution, or that they failed to consider the omnipotence of that God who is alone able to protect them."

In a free society, religious faith both guards against the agelessness of temptations while placing a governor motor on our Blessings of freedom. Today is no different than in the days of Washington. Let his words guide us through a glorious November. God Bless America.

Humor, Horror, or America?

July 13, 2012

For over three years now, the American public has been exposed to the quips from a Vice President whose conduct supports a growing belief that his selection was based more upon his value as a life insurance policy than his possible leadership capabilities. The latter category must be recognized simply based upon his "next in line" status. In reality, this bumpkin has been a politician, devoid of any "leadership" stirrings while cashing Federal paychecks and has only taken up space in the Senate chamber, period.

Given Biden's recorded CD of his three year misspeaks, if there actually was one, I would be remiss if I didn't recall how our truth-seeking media, during 2008, dissected every Palin reply while passing on "ole Joe's" treasure chest of verbal gaffs.

A passerby to the American politics may resign the office of the Vice Presidency to that of a needless necessity, given that it usually comes into play through assassinations or a resignation. Luckily, some of its occupants were never tested.

Probably the most famous, or most infamous, dance with lunacy came from that election cliff hanger when Al Gore finally took second place. However, this freed him up to follow further fame by inventing the internet and then by climbing the mountains, away from the heat of his lucrative campaign against global "warming." Few, including Gore, remembered back to the seventies when the polar ice caps were projected to threaten New York City. Today, it seems that many locations featuring a Gore seminar experience timely, and often unprecedented, snow falls. It has been said that "The Lord works in mysterious ways."

So, our vice-presidential rearview mirror may at times reflect a political symmetry between humor and horror. Currently, our bellies are sore from Biden's latest faux pas when speaking to a La Raza convention. I might caution those not in the gamesmanship of campaigning, that while Biden's actual appearance in front of an organization which identifies with the return of our southwestern States' to its Mexican roots may seem inappropriate, Vice Presidents are usually given a wide swathe, and especially so when the Vice President is Biden; since his "foot in mouth" flare often contributes to and/or makes up for "slow news days."

Can you believe that our VP, in an effort to be with people living a "thin wall" quarters, would detail his parent's buying of a thin-walled house in the mid-fifties, and then he proceeded to come out with, "wonder how my parents did it?"

For Biden, his future seems secure as these idiotic if not rude and/or disrespectful statements only add to his job security from a reversed perspective. Obama's second in command will never move up unexpectedly since his three-plus-year buffoonish record ensures his second-place finish. Ironically, it also ensures his renewal as Vice President if so, chosen by an equally dimwitted electorate.

Often, Biden's humor comes at a cost. I remember recently, he was introduced at a political rally and after taking the podium, he began to read off the list of those local political leaders who had a hand in the hosting of his event. Not to disappoint, as Biden read through this list, he came to "Chuck." In true Biden form and for some unknown reason, identifying this individual just didn't do it for our Vice President. No sir, in the midst of the usual round of applause, Biden had to say words to the effect of "Let's hear it for Chuck, stand up Chuck and take a bow". Now, I'm paraphrasing but that was the general call to action. Almost instantly, this nitwit realized that Chuck was in a wheelchair. He quickly reversed direction with his, and again I'm paraphrasing, "Oh my God, everyone stands up for Chuck."

Now gaffs happen. If it was a Democrat other than Biden, the matter would have been forgotten as is the usual case with Obama's coverage. But, the media, being the dogs that they are, have come to not only love Biden but to rely upon Biden. It's almost like a day without Biden is a day without sunshine. And through it all, Biden, in all his ignorant arrogance, eats it up!

So, the bottom line to all this is a dismal Obama/Biden report card. Up until today, our equally buffoonish President is apparently content with Biden remaining as a part of his re-election ticket. After all, his silver tongue appeal got him this far and Biden certainly didn't contribute. But how much can be tolerated and at what point is Biden's future cast in stone?

Consider one of Biden's more recent misspeaks. In a hotly contested campaign season and after three plus years of unproductive Presidential policies, especially regarding economic matters, Obama instinctively skirts any related question in almost the fashion of a Dracula avoiding sunlight.

In other words, we have an incumbent running for re-election who remains incapable of promoting his own Presidential record; especially so when the topic is America's economy and how he himself admitted that if it didn't rebound, he'd be a one-term President.

Enter Joe Biden, the clown, but also the insurance policy. What to do, how to help his boss gain renewed public confidence? I can just see Biden in a darkened corner say, "Gee, I know!" A light goes off in Biden's attic of a mind. He then jumps on Obama's political "third rail." Can you believe that Biden actually outdoes his "Stand up for Chuck" routine? How about classifying our economy, not as being in an upswing or even breaking out of a recession? No, the number two idiot has to rate our economy as a depression!

Ladies and gentlemen, if this wasn't such a serious election and the word "serious" doesn't even begin to describe what's at stake, Biden would be a standing room only attraction, somewhere. However, the horror of Obama's possible re-election cannot even be offset by the humor which we have come to expect from this Delaware clown.

Of course, contrary to Obama's 2008 infamous oratory acclaim, expressly yammered by our media punditry, he himself seems to be at odds with the English language and basic American History. Without detailing his personal list of misspeaks, one from each category may suffice.

How about pronouncing the term "medical corpsman" as "medical corpse man? I mean what American, fully versed in America's victorious and patriotically moving war movies cannot recall the yell for a corpsman to tend after a wounded buddy? Of course, maybe I assume too much. Our President just may not be able to watch a victorious and patriotic rendition of America while privately believing and condemning our Country as a "colonial" monster.

As for the second example, Obama infamously stated during his 2008 Presidential bid that so far, he has visited fifty-seven States. Again, I paraphrase but the "so far" and the number "fifty-seven" are accurate. Still, with the help of an apologetic media, he managed to become President.

Presenting this perspective is with the hope that it further cements our determination, even from somewhat of a lighthearted slant. While our situation is dire, the message herein reminds us that the magnitude of our former complacency actually produced the election of a serious threat and a serious buffoon. With this take in mind, who can argue with the obvious that the Obama Presidency was, as Dandy Don Meredith would say, "a hitch in our get along?"

That "hitch" caused our national Tea Party. In November, I'm betting that the electorate is fed up with both humor and horror. November's main feature may well return America's viewership to a long-awaited rerun of patriotism as America once again rises up triumphantly.

Everything Goes Around, Comes Around

July 14, 2012

Dear friends, even of the lifelong variety, have labeled me and my beliefs as being radical. I have worn this identity with pride since throughout my life; I have paddled against the current many times and in the right direction. This is one of those times.

Too often, modern day Americans refer to our Forefather's time as "back then" or "back when," as if to point out some cataclysmic separation, which forever distanced the bygone from the present. Usually, this viewpoint is falsely manufactured through a litany of references to modern day technology verses the well-worn "horse-and-buggy" theme.

One basic guideline to progressive thought is to first mislead. If that hook is snapped up, then all that follows takes place in their mental playground where discussions eventually wind up being moot. It's their technique by which the debate is controlled, and the outcome assured.

This ploy to control the exchange of ideas through diversion is simply a defensive mechanism since the progressive mind cannot cope with the facts spouted from the originalist platform. Theories wilt when faced with facts.

Those who work tirelessly to nitpick and/or re-interpret our Constitutional plain talk also refuse to admit that the basic premise adhered to by our Forefathers was to guard against the foible nature of the human species. In short, temptations are everlasting lures which may crumble any worthwhile endeavor. Government, even with our

Forefather's specific charge of limited power, remains particularly susceptible given man's natural inclination for power and control.

This, not the results from innovation, was and is what our Founding Fathers toiled to guard against. The progressive realizes this but remains adamant with his revisionist dogma. So, in order to clear the air and remain on target for this discussion, some of the words which ignited our drive for Independence are now noteworthy to consider, if only for their continued re-appearance and applicable appeal over time.

Before canvassing our precious beginnings, brought to us by Thomas Jefferson, it might be useful to critique our individual worthiness of the Blessings which our gallant Forefathers sacrificed in order to grant.

Who, in this modern era, would endure the many trials and tribulations which comprised our War for Independence? We seem to forget a major difference from our modern military sacrifices. Today, we defend what we possess and value. In their day, they sacrificed for a belief which had yet to be realized. Big difference.

For now, let's tie together that horse and buggy with our jet air travel through an understanding that human nature is ever present and unchanging.

Thomas Jefferson penned our Declaration and in doing so, listed injurious claims which, to that point, remained unaddressed; therefore, requiring a Declaration of Independence from those grievances. Consider their continuation into the modern era while echoing a sameness of tyrannical intent.

"He has refused his assent to laws the most wholesome and necessary for the public good."

"He has forbidden his governors to pass laws of immediate and pressing importance."

"He has dissolved representative houses repeatedly for opposing, with manly firmness, his invasions on the rights of the people."

"He has obstructed the administration of justice."

"He has erected a multitude of new offices, and sent hither swarms of officers, to harass our people, and eat out their substance."

"He has combined with others, to subject us to a jurisdiction foreign to our Constitution, and unacknowledged by our laws; giving his assent to their acts of pretended legislation."

"He has excited domestic insurrections among us."

These are just some of the many listed grievances which compelled our Forefather's course of action. Thomas Jefferson's Declaration concluded with what today may be deemed by some as "above and beyond." Their united belief and devotion to the unknown outcome of their cause inspires with the words, "And, for the support of this declaration, with a firm reliance on the protection of Divine Providence, we mutually pledge to each other our lives, our fortunes, and our sacred honor."

Our respect for what we've been bequeathed can be finely edged by brief excerpts from the Military Journal of the American Revolution, written by Dr. James Thacher, a surgeon with the Continental Army, and published by Corner House Historical Publications.

Dr. Thacher's War Journal entry on December 4th, 1775,

"A considerable number of Connecticut troops have left our service and returned home; no persuasion could induce them to continue in service after their time of enlistment has expired."

One last entry relates to the precariousness of our struggle against the mightiest military of the day. The December 11 entry informs:

"A party of militia, said to be about two thousand, have arrived in camp; and information is received that three thousand more are on their march. A few enlisted soldiers have arrived; but so destitute are they of firearms, that it has been found necessary to take the arms by force from the soldiers who retire, paying for them, in order to supply the recruits."

As we continue through with our daily schedules and individual routines, little regard is afforded to just what it required so that we may have and partake in the Blessings of our free society. Forcefully acquiring weapons, one at a time, in order to equip the soldiers, paints a picture of just how iffy our chances were of gaining freedom from oppression.

It seems that today, our predicament has come full cycle. Those injustices which Jefferson listed have resurfaced amid our push buttoned computerized existence. Imagine that Mr. Progressive!

The more that is read of our beginnings, the more parallels emerge. We today are the inheritors of a gallant heritage. Likewise, we are being tested by the same caliber of grotesque tyranny which our Forefathers confronted. Its tentacles are always there, in willing anticipation of the gullible and the weak.

May our prayers be heard so as to bring a victorious November. In similar Trenton fashion, another victory aided by Divine Providence, and praised around the world. God Bless America!

The Obama Magic

July 19, 2012

Obama's ego and inner angst is such that it will only be satisfied through his intent to heave insult after insult upon our American people and their Country. Track this man's continued assertions of America's ineptness. Imagine this against the most successful and prosperous country ever! Yes, he is a Marxist but also an ideologue who lacks any normal patience due to his inner calling.

Obama's narcissistic makeup drives his compulsion to both shred American independence and well-being but also to savor each industry's demise, each re-location so as to keep from an able-bodied American workforce.

His glee when envisioning his approaching re-election may have fed this personal release against free enterprise and in doing so, presents the American voter with quite an unpleasant future if Obama's vision becomes a reality.

Suffice to say that Obama has remained faithful to his life's quest of insuring a peaceful rest to his father's troubled and fruitless existence. Obama's schooling among his fellow anti-American associations focused his anti-capitalistic drive into that of a devoted Marxist. Adding vigor to his anti-American vendetta was the memory of his father's vent against America's supposed colonialism.

In his younger years, Obama preferred revolution as America's path for transforming. Along the way, he was exposed to the more patient tactic of achieving this radical upheaval by means of social and political reforms. This was suggested by student and fellow committed Marxist, John Drew.

Dr. John Drew has since left his days of Marxism far behind when long ago joining the ranks of conservative Americans; yet he is able to offer his private knowledge and insight of a younger Obama, from a time when he knew him as a devoted and consumed Marxist revolutionary.

On February 24, 2011, American Thinker published Dr. Drew's Meeting Young Obama. Its impact is immediate since at the time, Drew was in concert with that Marxist mindset. His message is from the inside of revolution, when plotting and designing against America was their cause. If I may, brief quotes from that essay should jolt some from their bewildered can do no wrong "messiah" daze.

Within this expose, Dr. Drew confesses that he "had been an angry Marxist revolutionary during his undergraduate career at Occidental College." Again, this admission certifies his insider credentials while also setting the stage for the players who entered. One of which is Obama.

Dr. Drew first met Obama in 1980. Obama arrived as a passenger in a fancy vehicle driven by Mohammed Hasan Chandoo, "a wealthy 21-year-old Pakistani student." Chandoo "was a socialist, a Marxist…" This took place at the family residence of Caroline Boss, Drew's girlfriend at the time, who was also active with her anti-American, pro-Marxist beliefs.

While all in attendance were of the same Marxist-Leninist beliefs for open or direct revolution, Drew had recently differed as he had come to believe that a more gradual, or within the system approach would be a better fit in a highly industrialized nation. Drew realized that "politics, rather than revolution, as the preferred route to socialism."

The following quotes taken from an after-dinner conversation may offend but hopefully enlighten. Drew writes, "Obama repeatedly used the phrase 'When the revolution comes…'" "Boss and Obama seemed to think their ideological purity was a persuasive argument in predicting that a coming revolution would end capitalism."

Drew's position was, "I responded it was unrealistic to think the working class would ever overthrow the capitalist system. As I recall, Obama reacted negatively to my critique, saying: 'That's crazy!'"

Finally, Dr. Drew writes, "I can state that everything I heard Obama argue that evening was consistent with Marxist philosophy, including the ideas that class struggle was leading to an inevitable revolution."

So, his current lecture of class differentiation actually reaches back to his 1980 beliefs. Now that he has captured the supreme seat of political power in America, his original revolutionary preference seems to still hold a firm appeal. Poverty brings desperation and desperation feeds susceptibility which in turn can lead to mass control.

To those who would point to Drew's recall as being approximately thirty years past, Obama's record in office is of the present. If it barks like a dog, smells like a dog and walks like a dog, it's a damn dog! Obama's policies, of which socialized health care was and now is his administration's so-called benchmark, should settle the debate.

From his earliest years, Obama was reared in the fabrics of socialism and Communism. His primary education lacked an American foundation since many of his years were in schools overseas. His significant role models were of the general anti-capitalist, anti-colonial mindset, if not being outright adherents to the socialist/communist creeds. His associates at Occidental College were of the same communist pedigree. Today, as president, his successful healthcare package bares his socialist core beliefs. Contrary to its misleading title, such care is merely a mask hiding an assault upon the hardworking American family.

America's strength has always been within its working/middle class citizens. It is here, among the blue collar ranks that the American fiber of freedom and individual opportunity is the strongest. This is the glue which binds America as she produces and builds her muscle and our unity and cohesiveness in times of emergency, peace and prosperity. As such, it provides our economic bulwark against the socialist themes offered by "the people's oppression."

Before Obama, America survived its ups and downs without any thought to class jealousy. Obama's current drive for re-election rehashes the same old communist dribble of class envy. He has remained stagnant and deeply rooted within that rebellious muck from his Occidental College days.

Consider his latest, as Obama just recently exclaimed, "If you've been successful, you didn't get there on your own. You didn't get there on your own. I'm always struck by people who think, 'Well, it must be because I was just so smart!'" Obama shows his delight with that well-worn communist refrain of the collective, while attacking individualism with his quip, "If you were successful, somebody along the line gave you some help."

Now, this is a President of the United States who is preaching this gibberish and not some down and out street corner hustler. He continues to astound working Americans with, "If you've got a business, you, you didn't build it."

Personally, I know a few self-made individuals who worked day and night, seven days a week to become successful and who would naturally take a very heated exception to Obama's prattle.

As former New Hampshire Governor John Sununu summed up recently, "These are the people who are the backbone of our economy and the president clearly demonstrated that he has absolutely no idea how the American economy functions." The former Governor added, in part, "…I wish this president would learn how to be an American."

We essentially have elected a person who is confident when showing off his American ignorance and loathing. It is this lifelong hatred of America which has finally caused him to flaunt his communist beliefs. Voters beware!

Romney's Betrayal

July 28, 2012

Romney is proving that his little pinky contains more Presidential timber than Obama's entire body. Even prior to his own nomination, he has scheduled a visit to our most trusted ally in the Middle East. By the way Obama, that happens to be Israel.

Along the way, a good-natured Romney thought it proper to stop by another trusted ally, Britain. Well, this spotty friend reverted back to its inherent colonial attitudes when confronted with another American upstart. By the way Obama, does our brief period of British servitude qualify America as a ranking member of the colonial victimization club?

Assuming he was in friendly territory, Romney answered honestly when being questioned by our media. Relying upon a kinship with Britain was his first mistake since the Brits have always been a thinned skinned lot with long memories. The second mistake was Romney's belief that Brian Williams was a fair and unbiased journalist. He's not! Williams is an attack dog out of the Obama puppy mill.

So, Williams queries Romney with the question, "In the short time you've been here in London, do they look ready for the Olympics to your experienced eye?"

In this setting, the honest businessman, not a career politician, answered. If his resume was of the latter, that loaded question, if it was even asked, would have been immediately ignored by a five-minute dissertation about how lovely London always is during the summer months; or some other dog droppings along those lines.

At any rate, Romney's response was apolitical and truthful. To quote, "You know, it's just hard to know just how well it will turn out. There are a few things that were disconcerting, the stories about the private security firm not having enough people, the supposed strike of the immigration and customs officials. That obviously is not something which is encouraging."

Now, in a world of terrorist threats galore, Romney is not concerned with having enough personnel at the popcorn booth. One would think that although his truthful statement was blunt, it was worth nothing rather than attacking. Of course, now, we are conversing with the superior British mindset which continues to see the world through a pair of British skivvies. Never-the-less, the opportunity presented itself. A mad journalistic dash ensued. Abiding by the traditions of a "spinning press," headlines such as, "Romney struggles to stem fallout" greeted the morning coffee sippers.

What is telling throughout this blown-up article is the honesty with which our next president expresses. Regardless of feelings or politically correct expectations, when one reads down from the headline to Romney's reply, it will hit the reader like a ton of bricks. At last, honesty!

This AP release, written by Steve Peoples and Kasie Hunt is typical of the spinning that has converted news reporting into editorializing. Amid the opening paragraph, readers are treated with the assumption that Romney's answer was actually a "stumble." This is classic spin since to view an honest reply as a "stumble" necessitates imposing one's impression instead of what actually took place. Also, in that paragraph was the bloviated view that Romney's reply "pitted" him "against America's strongest ally." History tells a different version.

Who came to the aide of whom in WWII? Where was our "strongest ally" during the wars in Korea and Vietnam? And of course, what has been "Great" Britain's percentage of military backing since 9/11?

What really strikes out as being sinister, from a perspective of political loyalty, if in fact that term isn't actually an oxymoron, what really stands out is that rock of loyalty, Karl Rove, as he once again reveals an alternate agenda by his Fox News remark, "You have to shake your head." As always, the lead RINO with his subtle innuendos.

I mean, here is Rove's reaction to Romney's honest appraisal of the British's Olympics preparedness. Is this the voice of conservative thought, one who supposedly dodged all the arrows against the Bush Administration? How can the "architect" of the Republican Party talk in such iffy terms about the candidate who has been chosen to dethrone Obama? Forget party loyalty; tell me the purpose which the comment, "You have to shake your head" serves? The obvious intent is to weaken Romney support!

And another point for considering is why this British push for keeping Romney's assessment in the limelight? One would think that a true "ally" would give cover to a misspeak, or just leave it fade away. Especially so when considering who in all probability will be the next American President. Could it be that Britain is quite satisfied with another four years of Obama?

What emerged in 2010 and continues to the present is the public's realization that the media (MSM) is anything but a "free press." At best, it is a liberal mouthpiece, and at worst, an accomplice to all of Obama's past, present and future Constitutional injustices. This AP "hit" piece detailing Romney's honest judgment to what he witnessed is a last ditched attempt to minimize the positives from Romney's overseas tour.

Ironically, his three Country tour has already accomplished the impossible since Obama has allocated approximately fifty million dollars in aid to Israel. Without this overseas jaunt, highlighted by Romney's visit to a country which Obama has yet to see as an American President, this generosity would have never taken place.

It remains as a sore and embarrassing point that as President, Obama has yet to visit our "strongest ally" in the Middle East. Especially since as a candidate he did so during his own pre-election version of bolstering his foreign affairs acumen. While traveling about during that 2008 overseas journey, Obama committed more than a misspeak of a sporting event. However, his major faux pas went unnoticed as the 2008 Obama protection racket, afforded by our MSM was in full gear. Briefly, what follows may extinguish this recent Romney blowup.

From a brief New York Post report, written by Iraqi born Amir Taheri, then Senator Obama privately attempted to postpone an agreement on a partial withdrawal of American troops till after the new administration takes office in January. Obviously, Obama viewed this to be an advantageous credit to his expected young Presidency. This was a subject supposedly discussed privately between Obama and Iraqi foreign minister Hoshyar Zebari.

Let's see, the use of our military as political pawns verses the truthful but blunt answer to a valid question. This is the type of media protection which Obama continues to enjoy. Furthermore, it will be interesting to compare the present media coverage from Britain verses the coverage of Romney's upcoming warm Israeli welcome.

Romney's overseas trip has revealed the usual domestic culprits since the RINO's mouthpiece, Karl Rove, does not bark without command. Rove's telling remark cannot be emphasized enough. It captures another hidden Republican spirit, one cradled by their "Establishment" and one which seeks to preserve business as usual. In this case, it's not the businessman but the Marxist who has been chosen to continue their bidding. Mischief often demands strange bedfellows.

Softness of Our Chains

October 8, 2012

It's not like we all go through life without making wrong judgments or mistakes. That's life! In fact, mistakes provide us with our most efficient learning lessons. So, how is it that a substantial amount of American voters, having endured nearly four years of economic decline, foreign setbacks and inept leadership cannot agree with the obvious conclusion that, yes, we made a mistake?

Mistakes are everywhere in life. Probably our most important decision comes in the choosing of our life partner. Statistics reveal that roughly one out of every two marriages end up in divorce. Whatever the reasons, we deal with our misfortunes and survive to another day, and maybe even another spouse.

While marriage is probably the most important, everyday judgments can roughly follow this fifty-fifty decision-making average. The point is that we cope and learn from life's many lessons. So, what makes our Presidential pick so hard to reverse? Not for all of us, but certainly for many.

This stubborn refusal defies our natural human instincts of reasoning and overcoming. As a rule of thumb, those who refuse irrefutable facts, facts which present a clear choice, do so at least partially, from an influence which in this case, is affecting the scales of human potential and prosperity.

Consider buying a fancy car which turns out to be a lemon, or a house which has leaks in the roof when it rains. As these setbacks become obvious, our learning instincts automatically devalue the fancy appeal when purchasing our next vehicle. Many who move a second time do so after checking out their next house in rainy weather! We learn.

So, this refusal to admit that "yes, I made a mistake," may well elevate emotion over practical reasoning. Obama is a gifted puller of heart strings. His oratory skills are best directed at the crowd he is pleasing rather than defending his record. His verbal appeal is packed with emotional tugs which temper listeners from using any comparative or independent judgments. As such, his Presidential accountability gets a pass.

Considering his style of governance, his current use of division, unrest and public dependency serves to camouflage a disastrous record. Even his most monumental achievement, universal healthcare legislation, was rammed through our Congress with bribes, coercion and false promises. It mattered little that the American people were against this takeover of America's medical industry. As he once remarked, "I'm not just a candidate, I'm the president."

Loyalty to a belief, even a political one is understandable, but only to a point. However, country comes before party loyalty simply based upon the fact that without our Country, the party is where? So, we can afford to lose a party but not a Country.

Way back in our earlier years, many of today's voters were unaware of the complete ruination of our sound and useful form of education. Even in my day, fundamental subjects basically remained, and George Washington's portrait hung on every classroom wall. For too many generations, that traditional American curriculum has been pasteurized and our Founding Father's eliminated. This is not debatable, yet the average citizen and parent remain unaware.

What do we expect from each generation if, in their most formative years, they are subjected to the dribble which now is espoused? This anti-American mantra is the instruction given to those we supposedly treasure and love the most! May I ask, "What the hell are we doing as parents?"

Given the fact that the federal government lacks any education authority, how can we expect a different or more balanced educational product? After all, too much education would produce a more questioning electorate. As previously noted, our un-American sentiment is nurtured during our formal education years and our stampede into "higher learning" only accelerates and finely tunes this destructive venue.

Now consider our American experiment and judge for yourself how terrible it is. All our angst has been inspired from a juggernaut of socialistic reasoning that must use impoverishment in order to grow. We are currently doing the devil's work as we seek to degrade every aspect of the American ideal.

Is America perfect? Hell no! But show me another place which comes close to matching our freedoms, success or living standards. Get away from your emotional idealisms and start making a plus versus minus list. Get down to the basics in order to get past this anti-American crap!

Think of the divisive spiel which consumes the majority of Obama's campus speeches. This President shies away from the knowledgeable or experienced voter. He feels most at ease on the college tour and finds his success through derisive commentary. His appeal is to an audience lacking comparative judgment simply because of their youth.

Again, think about what it means for us, to be led by a President who declares that "America is not a Christian nation." Do we really feel comfortable in voting for an un-American? There can only be one interpretation from his quip, "If congress will not act, I will." The man is without any merit as he routinely ignores the legal limitations of his office.

In closing, this election is not based upon politics. This is the frontal assault from the enemies of American capitalism and freedom. Going out to vote is now in defense of our Country since these people are here and they are serious!

Our Fundamental Return

December 29, 2012

An appropriate comparison could be when the Indians chased the buffalo over the cliff versus this current version which stampedes the American mind into confusion, disorder and then finally into a state of compliance without any thought or hesitation.

Also, this parade of modern time saving conveniences have eased our physical toil while still managing to negatively affect our well-being as our brand of Americanism fades in proportion of our distancing from faith, morality, societal cohesiveness and America's "can do" spirit. Such abandonment has introduced idleness, boredom, jealousy, indifference and self-interest.

In testament to their far sightedness, it was this eventuality to which our Forefathers directed their most ardent attention. Probably, Daniel Wedster best described what the above passages attempted. Our current condition was eerily forecasted when he stated the following:

"Our destruction, should it come at all, will be from another quarter. From the inattention of the people to the concerns of their government, from their carelessness and negligence, I must confess that I do apprehend some danger. I fear that they may place too implicit a confidence in their public servants and fail properly to scrutinize their conduct. That in this way they may be made the dupes of designing men and become the instruments of their own undoing."

While not mentioned, Webster's concerns may be related to our current exclusion of our Christian doctrines.

Webster's words also lend credence to our Founder's words in our Bill of Rights. What impresses is the overall "cannot" theme. Their opening words to the First Amendment strictly inform that, "Congress shall make no law…" Certainly, their emphasis in our Second Amendment, "shall not be infringed," carries this "cannot" theme as does the Fourth's "shall not be violated."

Their recognition of God given "unalienable" rights all served one purpose; that these Rights were above man's "mischief." Since our Founding Fathers all reasoned that men were not angels, they embarked upon the impossible mission of creating a government with enough authority to restrict yet able to protect without any potential for abuse. Contrary to the left's charge of it being "a negative charter," it's just the opposite!

In full recognition of man's shortcomings, our magnificent Forefathers constructed a government bent on limitations while at the same time offering its citizens the greatest sanctioned field for opportunity, self-determination and freedom from interference.

It is interesting to note that our band of freedom writers also reflected the essence of positive thinking. They acknowledged man's shortcomings yet, as James Madison so eloquently remarked:

"We have staked the whole future of American civilization, not upon the power of government, far from it. We have staked the future of all of our political institutions upon the capacity of mankind for self-government; upon the capacity of each and all of us to govern ourselves, to control ourselves, to sustain ourselves according to the Ten Commandments."

The basis for Madison's address was in the fact that the American society of his day was staunchly versed and obedient to the Scriptures of Christianity.

And it is with those words of Madison that our present mess may be addressed. What has happened didn't occur over night so its cure will not be quick. Ours has been a gradual and unnoticeable road, but still, similar to the hands of a clock, eventually very telling. Today is our telling hour.

Merely a mending here and there of our Nation's missteps is ineffectual when facing America's institutionalized feeding of indifference and apathy. Our remedies can only be from our

Constitution since it was then that our government was most stable and weaved its finest thread.

Whether it be the devastating effects from the passage of the Seventeenth Amendment, the irresponsibility from undeclared wars, the various unconstitutional Supreme Court decisions, most notably, when outlawing school prayer and devaluing precious life, or when government taxes anything which moves or breaths, much awaits our correcting before our America returns to Her independent and productive "can do" self.

A companion with today's innovative swirl is this anti-American trend of secularism, which has transcended from its former hallucinogenic cloud into a societal voice. If our critical reformation proceeds upon the basis of our Christian beginnings, we automatically can identify secularism as major factor to our disunity. This point was enforced when our Supreme Court, in its 1963 School District of Abington Township v. Schempp declared, "Secularism is unconstitutional."

Equal to its role during our struggle for Independence and later at our Constitutional Convention, Christianity acted both as an aid for conducting a productive debate, and later for binding our societal harmony.

The overall benefit from our Christian foundation is the inner stabilization which tempers the elected and restrains citizens into a more respectful and congenial co-existence. Our first President, George Washington, said it best about our Blessings from faith: "true religion affords to government its surest support."

In a lighter tone, as New Years Eve approaches, the letters "CC" usually are associated with that tasty import from up north, Canadian Club whisky. Maybe we could kick off this New Year with our own domestic CC brand; Christianity mixed equally with our Constitution!

Something Evil Came Our Way

January 10, 2013

Let it be said that we have embraced a glib, smooth-talking interloper who managed to gain our public's trust. His re-election now stands out as a testament to our inner thoughts and wants to be manipulated into accepting what in former times would be considered an unworthy candidate. And this isn't the first time!

Human animals are capable of thought and by its process, forms likes and dislikes, akin to our individual ice cream favorites. This ability prompts our species to excel in all endeavors. These traits are part of our "human nature" and it is to this complexity which our Forefather directed much of their astute judgments.

Our Founders realized that our superior human animal was Blessed with abilities which could service needs and initiate improvements while also owning nature's inherent frailties. Therefore, our Forefathers agreed that if men were angels, government would not be necessary. Thus, since angels they were not, they sought to write what they thought would best serve against the more tempting side of nature.

To set the stage, Benjamin Franklin stated, "Let me add that only virtuous people are capable of freedom. As nations become corrupt and vicious, they have more need of masters." Also mindful to consider, when confronted by today's secular influences, are the words from another Founding Father, James Monroe. In his first inaugural address, President Monroe stated in part:

> "It is only when the people become ignorant and corrupt,
> when they degenerate into a populace, that they are

incapable of exercising sovereignty. Usurpation is then an easy attainment, and a usurper soon found. The people themselves become the willing instruments of their own debasement and ruin."

Far sighted they were!

We have "soon found" our present-day usurper. And as our Founding Fathers so plainly described, we are now the "populace" which seems unworthy of "exercising the sovereignty." As a matter of fact, and supportive with this conclusion, most modern-day Americans couldn't begin to explain what "exercising the sovereignty" means!

So, as Mr. Benjamin Franklin pointed to "only a virtuous people," and President Monroe mentioned "when the people become ignorant and corrupt," I think today's situations have been first instigated and then beset by what has been best identified as "usurpers."

Enter modern-day government. The last century can best be described as an onslaught against our Forefathers beliefs. The latest attack, and probably the boldest and far reaching, has sadly been re-elected. In a sad admission, he is but the latest to extricate themselves from "the chains of the Constitution." (Thomas Jefferson, TJ, quote)

More recently, we find ourselves swept along with what happened at a grade school in Connecticut prior to our Christmas joy. Since that dreadful event, our front pages have been filled with the gruesome and often minute detailing of the tragedy's aftermath. However, within hours of that tragedy, Obama callously voiced his usurpation intent as part of a national speech.

The official definition of an "opportunist" is as follows: "One who takes advantage of an opportunity to achieve an end, often with no regard for principles or consequences." This one insensitive performance may forever label this President and his Presidency as owning the usurper tagline!

Since Obama's original election, the American voter has been fed one lie after another. The $1 trillion "stimulus" bill actually failed to stimulate. In response, the President laughingly remarked, "those jobs weren't as shovel ready as I thought." This may not be so comical for those seeking employment.

Now we are told that Obamacare will somehow pick up an additional thirty to fifty million uninsured despites being billed as "free healthcare." Who is it that pays? Forget that its pages remained unread and that it "had to be passed to find out what's in it." I may have paraphrased but we all are familiar with Pelosi's insult, which has sadly become a government routine. This infers that their regard is with informing their subjects after, rather than before, when citizens are their sovereign employers.

Still, this insufferable record takes second place to what is now being previewed by the most useless Senator and now that most do-nothing Vice President in American history. Biden now publicly ponders whether he will either write an executive order outlawing our Second Amendment or piecemeal it out of existence.

This attitude and expectation must alert and unite Americans, regardless of political ideologies! What we are talking about is an out-of-control public servant who somehow thinks that he can legislate without Congress. But more than that, he conceives his authority to be at a higher level than that of our Creator. We now must ask, "what the hell is next?"

Our Bill of Rights is a list of ten unalienable rights from our Creator and bequeathed to us at the time of our birth. As such, they are set above the "mischief of man," (TJ). If at any time there could be reasoning which would justify the challenging of these God given rights, which is inconceivable, the only possible way to re-write or eliminate any Amendment is through our Amendment process. To suggest otherwise, based upon one's oath of office, is a criminal act!

Much has been lost or given away from our original prescription of freedom. In Washington's Farewell Address, he cautions that, "reason and experience both forbid us to expect that national morality can prevail in exclusion of religious principle." Thus, basic education during our Founding Era and long afterward included religious instruction.

As we face further attempted usurpations of our freedoms and unalienable rights, especially with our current concern for our Second Amendment, I reference a Jefferson letter he wrote to his nephew in 1785 which included the subject of personal exercise. He mentioned that two hours per day should be allotted and that, "as to the species of exercise, I advise the gun. While this gives moderate exercise to the body, it gives boldness, enterprise, and independence to the mind."

St. George Tucker, authored the first legal treatise on the Constitution, and which became the legal text lasting well into the nineteenth century, he wrote,

> "This may be considered as the true palladium of liberty…The right of self-defense is the first law of nature, in most governments it has been the study of rulers to confine this right within the narrowest limits possible."

He also wrote that,

> "The congress of the United States possesses no power to regulate, or interfere with the domestic concerns, or police of any state: it belongs not to them to establish any rules respecting the rights of property; nor will the constitution permit any prohibition of arms to the people."

Although not well known, Tucker is not to be taken lightly. He was a Founding Father, a leading Constitutional scholar and author, best remembered for his View of the Constitution of the United States, the previously cited text, published in 1803 and which was widely relied upon by legal minds of that time and afterwards.

Lastly, I refer to these quotes for their substance of being from the original mindset and purpose of our Forefathers. Our Founding words and beliefs were relied upon then and were responsible for our National acclaim, independence and prosperity. So, why are such words not relevant today?

One Identified RINO

February 15, 2013

I assume that many of us hold dear the words and sentiments from a favored columnist. For me, it was the Philadelphia Inquirer's Darrell Sifford. Mr. Sifford died well over twenty years ago. His syndicated columns focused upon life and the differing relationships and dilemmas which we all must deal with.

Today, as syndication has been kidnapped by liberal political theorists for the most part, many take delight in finding the few remaining writers who bolster our beliefs and positions. The scarcity of this particular field of written thought has brought an adjustment from our normal conservative standards to a sort of elasticity as journalists have now attempted to sway our morning thoughts leftward. When realizing this, it then becomes insufferable when one of "our own" reliable journalists disappoint. This recently took place with Cal Thomas' latest effort.

Thomas' faux pas was not from the innocuous inclusion of a one liner or a single phrase in an otherwise conservative column. In this particular case, the theme throughout his article demonstrated qualities which will now alter my opinion and reading habits away from his essays to the point that I consider him to be a sham, a plant and most of all now, an identified member of the establishment's army of RINOs.

The title of Thomas' writing, "Political rant undermined an event meant to celebrate unifying faith" appeared under the critical heading of "Inappropriate Lecture." Obviously, the intent of the article was to condemn Dr. Benjamin Carson's oratory at the National Prayer Breakfast, held in Washington DC last week.

Thomas' opening paragraph describes the ambush of an American President, while attending what he considers to be "an event devoted to drawing people closer to God and bridge partisan and cultural divides without being lectured about his positions." To that I remark, "since when has Obama been so identified with such spiritual leanings and pursuits?" Should I add that Rev. Wright sermons do not qualify?

As already stated, Thomas' attack upon free speech and truth qualifies for his revised identity with the traitorous moniker of RINO. And he takes delight with his expansion of his anti-American notions throughout his piece while completely ignoring the fact that what the Doctor detailed was truthful and accurate.

Thomas attempts to dilute his criticism by writing that, "I am no fan of the president's policies, but the NPB is billed as one of the few nonpolitical events..." WOW! Are we to consider the sacrilege committed by Dr. Carson? Well Mr. Thomas, balance the sanctity of the NPB versus the higher sanctity of our Constitution!

A few excerpts from this article should aptly place Thomas on the wrong side of conservative America and forever ID the writer's true pedigree.

First, "his remarks were inappropriate...The president had a right to expect a different message..." Really? Could it be that Dr. Carson was attempting the rare feat of introducing Obama to the concept of being accountability for one's actions?

Essentially, "the president" is limited to the same rights as afforded to the average citizen. He is not worshipped or bowed down to as a king. As one of the inheritors of Obama's plan for taking America down to her economic knees, this dressing down by Dr. Carson was not only long overdue but, in all probability, I recognized and accepted this occasion as the only venue in which our grievances could be set forth and endured by such an elusive President.

Thomas naively writes that if Carson "wanted to voice his opinion...he could have done so backstage." Again, really? What is Obama, just hanging around? How does one approach let alone get a chance to converse? Thomas' suggestion of such a nonsensical option runs counter to the average citizen's understanding of this President's record for availability and openness. By writing such foolishness, he suggests a gullibility factor rooted at the grade school level of youthful innocence.

Finally, "Carson should publicly apologize…" For what? What he said was the truth and what Obama has produced during these past four years is diametrically opposite to what he promised. Not only has Obama worsened a serious financial situation, but he has also violated law after law in doing so. What is there to apologize for? The act of apologizing should come from Obama, not from Dr. Carson.

If we continue with that last quote, the entire sentence will reveal and forever plant Thomas in the RINO cornfield as it shines the light on the left's true dilemma pertaining to Dr. Carson's message. He and his commonsense oratory are to be both guarded against and publicly limited.

Again, Thomas sternly cautions Dr. Carson to, "Carson should publicly apologize and stop going on TV doing 'victory laps' and proclaiming that reaction to his speech was overwhelmingly positive." Therein lies the crux of the matter. The truth has always been inciting. Here was a doctor of international renown, upstaging an American President. And the truth is not only demanding. It's instinctively recognizable and addictive. Also, how dare he, not only a black doctor but more importantly, a black conservative, appear so insolent, maybe even defiant, with the president nearby?

The truth of the matter is that Obama filters every public appearance. News conferences are prearranged with certain questions already filtered and waiting to be queried. The chance of a "chance interview" is rare and when it does occur, Obama's responses are evasive, dismissive or just outright lies.

So, Dr. Carson seized the moment. Obama, at long last, was unable to ignore or evade his truthful message. I only wish that the good doctor included a couple of direct questions. I mean, if you are going to be a bear, you might as well be a grizzly!

One last comment to this RINO's "not playing fair' article. It hurts when the tables of control are reversed. Thomas writes, "Organizers for this event tell speakers ahead of time to steer clear of politics, but Carson apparently 'went rogue.'" One can bet that in the future, the leash will be ever so much tighter with regards to the parameters of available subject matter to be discussed.

Finally, is this to be the final resting place for truth today? It's rogue? Apparently, since Thomas' written reaction accurately portrays the media's overall regard. This, in part, substantiates our current distaste for the media's slanted and belittling overall quality, and why our condemnation has reached unprecedented levels.

Thusly, Thomas' column has inadvertently been beneficial, in that his writing validates our rebuke of the media and in doing so, he has flushed out his true identity. Someone should inform Mr. Thomas that contrary to his strident column, more will be heard from Dr. Benjamin Carson and his return will not be limited to such a constrained and pray-based venue.

Washington Still Leads

February 20, 2013

Friday, February 22nd, will be George Washington's 281st birthday; our greatest American President, born in 1732 and passed away December 14, 1799. During those all too brief sixty-seven years, what a magnificent life! So why is it that modern-day America seems so bent upon either ignoring or denying Washington's greatness?

Again, as inheritors of his greatness, his love of country over self-interests, his duty over ease and leisure and his humbled honor over man's shortcomings, why is it that America's official recognition is just about non-existent? Could the standards of conduct Washington bestowed truly be "out of sync" or incompatible with modern living? If so, what can be said of people who have become so crass?

It's interesting to note this sudden attention to President Lincoln. Isn't it odd that Spielberg would select Lincoln over the "do or die" adventures which largely adorned Washington's life? Not to take anything away from "Honest Abe," but really, if truth be known, George Washington came as close as any American has to being a true Superman!

One such example of his invincibility was retold in David Barton's account entitled The Bulletproof George Washington. A twenty-three-year-old Washington was at one time a Colonel with a British Army. During one particular battle against French and Indian forces, Washington was the only officer to have remained on horseback from a total of eighty-six. Of those, sixty-three became casualties. Years later, an Indian chief from that battle recounted that Washington, despite being specifically targeted, remained unscathed and thus the Indian chief considered that he (Washington) was "the man who is the particular favorite of Heaven, and who can never die in battle."

Whether it be a young British officer or the commander of the American army, General Washington led from the front, ahead of his troops. He had a number of horses shot out from under him and it was said that his uniforms totaled double digit bullet holes, all missing their mark.

Highly successful movies of epic proportions have been based upon much less. So, it remains befuddling as to why the adventurous deeds of Washington never made it to the big screen. Parallel this void with public education's complete disregard. What is more required for the forming of a conspiratorial web?

What best to read on February 22 than Washington himself? In a letter to his younger brother, he wrote, "I heard the bullet's whistle, and, believe me, there is something charming in the sound."

From his General Orders issued on July 2, 1776, He wrote,

"The time is now near at hand which must probably determine, whether Americans are to be, Freeman, or Slaves…The fate of unborn Millions will now depend, under God, on the Courage and Conduct of this army…We have therefore to resolve to conquer or die…and if we now shamefully fail, we shall become infamous to the whole world."

Also contained within his General Order,

"Let us therefore animate and encourage each other, and shew the whole world, that a freeman contending for Liberty on his own ground is superior to any slavish mercenary on earth."

Our Forefathers knew well that by signing the Declaration of Independence and from those opening volleys of rifle fire at Concord and Lexington, subsequent actions and strife would either result in freedom or death. Washington said as much in his July 2nd Order that, "We have therefore to resolve to conquer or die."

Today, our number one battle revolves around which political party will triumph. Pretty self-serving when compared with our Founding ordeals. In his Farewell Address on September 19, 1796, Washington cautioned about "the spirit of the party." Washington said:

"This spirit, unfortunately, is inseparable from our nature… The alternate domination of one faction over another, sharpened by the spirit of revenge natural to party dissention… is itself a frightful despotism…It serves always to distract the Public Councils and enfeeble the Public Administration. It agitates the Community with ill-founded jealousies and false alarms, kindles the animosity of one part against another."

Need I ask as to the relevance of Washington's warnings? What is the level of our unity today? Are we agitated by parties? Added to that state is the further unsettling from special interests. Our modern-day dithers are self-destructive and anyone who fuels these embers of agitation is in full knowledge and awareness of the probable outcomes; especially so when it originates from our own leadership sources.

And speaking of that source, we have been told that America "is not a Christian nation." Our Founding Fathers entertained a different opinion.

As one of the founding Justices of our Supreme Court, Chief Justice John Marshall observed of Washington, "Without making ostentatious professions of religion, he was a sincere believer in the Christian faith, and a truly devout man."

As such, Washington's farewell included his belief that, "of all the dispositions and habits which lead to political prosperity, Religion and morality are indispensable supports." Once again, Washington leads with his advice for what is currently required for our reclaiming of America.

Finally, from his farewell speech, Washington proudly claimed that

> "The name of AMERICAN, which belongs to you, in
> your national capacity, must always exalt the just pride
> of patriotism, more than any appellation derived from
> local discriminations."

Our first President, one who refused a kingship, offers guidance for our proud reclaiming of the name AMERICAN. That identity, along with Washington's, has been desecrated for too long. So, on February 22nd, let us all say a prayer to our Creator and give an upward wink to that magnificent warrior and Statesman. We have so much to be thankful for but more importantly, so much that we must jealously guard and protect from enemies both foreign and domestic!

Orchestrating Free Elections

March 22, 2013

Thinking back to those 2012 Republican primary days, I can remember questioning just how we arrived with this slate of candidates. Who or what did the selections? Given the dreadful November results, which one must assume hinged greatly upon our final champion, I am now more aware, curious and if possible, protective of this protracted process. And today, the solemnity of my morning coffee was shattered by what appears to be the opening salvo of the 2016 contest.

The bold headlines read, "Clinton leads Bush, Rubio in matchups in 2016 Florida poll." This news flash carries the intention of suggestion as it tends to plant the "front runner" seed into the public's consciousness. Take it to the bank; this is the format for that final slate of candidates and in no way should it be given credence. Ladies and gentlemen, we are being played three years and eight months before the game!

This "early bird" snippet screams many indignities. First, the three designees are in no way front runners. One comes from a family which may be deemed "enough already." And just how many Bushes does America need and do we really expect anything different from this latest Bush sub?"

Secondly, Rubio was thrown in the mix to placate his Tea Party supporters. If truth be known, and if he should ever gain the nomination, you can bet the farm that our investigative media will make it known, he, is unqualified to run since he is not a "natural born citizen." Contrary to the media's deaf ears when this question arose concerning Obama, two wrongs don't make a right and one can be assured that our media will point this out once his nomination is secured.

Thirdly, and most insultingly, Clinton proved her unworthiness with her lack of "anything" regarding Benghazi. Her record of nothing is a lifetime accomplishment, ruefully highlighted by her recent, "at this point, what difference does it make" comment concerning the deaths of four Americans!

This AP article, written by Brent Kallestad, quoted Quinnipiac (Conn.) University Polling Institute's assistant director, Peter Brown as saying, "Florida voters have a very positive view of Mrs. Clinton, and it's not just Democrats who feel that way." Really?

If the writer of this sham would allow any acknowledgement of Dr. Carson to creep into his early matchups, his written findings of this tomfoolery survey become askew. And that's just one early surprise to what this and future prognosticators will face in our 2016 journey. Very telling is his ability to select the two most electable republicans this early. I suppose the writer is unaware of Senator Paul, who is just one of many young Constitutionalists to have corralled the public's attention.

Once again, this article's pro-Clinton flare demonstrates the establishment's low esteem for the values of the American public since this insult comes so closely on the heels of Ms. Clinton's pathetic Benghazi testimony. It may well be the writer's attempt to bury what he hopes to be just a bump in the road.

Floridians should inform Mr. Kallestad that similar to the rest of the nation, our "positive view" also shines upon Dr. Ben Carson and his penchant for logical review, especially when face to face with the one most responsible for this economic calamity.

Also pertinent to this question of early front runners is the recent admission that Dr. Carson would seriously consider a presidential run if the situation presented itself. Obviously, Dr. Carson's surprising entrance onto the national political scene is just one of the intangibles or unknowns which have yet to occur during this span of years. The minor item of "midterms" will also weigh heavily, after which we will up our attentions a notch higher towards 2016.

So, out of all the hundreds of millions of Americans, the process of selection now begins offensively with its premature designation of just three possibilities. Certainly, at this point, the field should be open and if not, how can our elections be truly "free?"

Our media outlets are busy at work, trying to ensure that their unethical mischief continues so as to assure that this socialistic trend continues into its final culmination. This is the course which was charted long ago and can be traced throughout the media's own trail of detailing its favorites.

This insult which was passed off as a probable 2016 presidential list of leading contenders presents the perfect example of just how our decisions are being engineered. This is what will greet the voters every morning till the 2016 election. It is the workings of an anti-American machine, intent upon limiting our voting options.

Dr. Ben Franklin famously responded, when asked about America's new government, "A Republic, if you can keep it." Such a premature and limited selection of candidates is not the makings of a healthy Republic. And the lack of any citizen push back is exactly what Dr. Franklin warned against so long ago!

Our Plate Silently Overflows

April 1, 2013

Have our manners of disrespect and apathy become so engrained that we now accept the disloyalty of nine mortals in black robes? Similar to those nine jurists, we also possess all the various human tendencies which tease at our weaknesses of temptation, jealousy and greed. Yet are we so dismissive of our American bedrock that we become resigned to their Constitutional contradictions? And just when did our Founding Fathers reassign legislation's authority from Congress to nine fallible individuals: or more to the point, from a Constitutional Republic to an oligarchy?

Marriage used to be one of those rocks. Today, the perversion of thought has dissected every truth into a microcosm of interrelated confusions and contradictions. This is the mess which shreds the whole through its own minute attentions. Is this recently devised equality quest so pressing that we are now able to discount centuries of proven customs, traditions, religious tenets and Constitutional law? If we untie the solemn state of matrimony, what absolutes can remain untouched?

This current questioning of marriage, as insipid and immoral as it obviously is, was always "waiting in the wings" from when gayness shed its closeted existence. Likewise, the signal was loud when Washington felt the need to defend the state of matrimony during the Clinton years, certainly an eerie beckoning given that particular President's penchant for cigars and other pastimes.

Initial gay arguments began with the well-meaning venues of "we are all human beings" and/or "we aren't second class citizens." Such pleas for human respect and decency, while being desirous, were in themselves argumentative, given the context in which they were presented. However, this posturing always accompanied a forum which was designed to eventually take on marriage's traditional and legal tenets.

In retrospect, those initial requests for "gay" recognition were similar to the cry detailing the injustices nonsmokers had to endure during air travel. Both voiced well-meaning objections which even amassed support from the ranks of its opposition.

However, as with any successful protest, each triumph necessitated another round. Today, the protests over those partitioned plane interiors have matured into encompassing the windblown expanses of our Nation's beaches as well as those calling for gay recognition have now grown into demands which entertain the desecration of the traditional marriage.

Common sense and concrete legal tenets have felt the slurs from this breed of domestic insurgency. We are at a precipice comparable to what our school children experience. It's called intimidation. The schoolyard bully now masquerades as the aggrieved litigant. Minority grievances abound and we genuflect accordingly. To what end will our eventual fate rest, given this intimidation and our preferred silence?

Our long season of silence seems never ending. Consider back to a time when prayer in school was offensive to a few. In what has become its sad unconstitutional logo, our Supreme Court banned prayer from the classroom. Lately, complaints against signs wishing a "Merry Christmas," have been filtered into "happy holidays." Nativity scenes face removal when agitated voices are heard. Consider the recent headlines announcing the need for "religious diversity" at an elementary school in Alabama. It seems that the word "Easter" hampers that school's attempt to "respect and honor everybody's differences."

That short quote says it all! Since when was America's "melting pot" transformed into a national cause for promoting "differences?" How in hell can America remain "united" when this diversity chant resounds? This challenges our American makeup, our very identity. As such, it must be addressed for the disjointedness it presents.

As a liberty based Christian Nation, our heritage has always extended the branch of religious freedom to all denominations and in doing so, further cemented our own religious grants. However, this acknowledgement does not endorse a basis of equality which would contend with; even possibly exclude our many forms of expression and worship. If this diversity claim continues, our freedom of religion will be reduced to closed-door gatherings. Obviously, this was not the First Amendment's intent!

By following this line of abstract thought, are we to understand that we should refrain from outward Christian displays since it would offend believers of other faiths? America was founded in Christianity, period. As other religions are free to be worshipped, they are to co-exist without demanding restrictions upon our Christian expressions of worship; highlighting "differences," to the exclusion of others, ridicules the role of individual rights. Our unalienable rights remain supreme and in this American "melting pot," differences are recognized solely as the weave of the American fabric.

There seems to be an organized effort against Christianity taking place right before our very eyes. For the most part, we either disbelieve or just ignore its encroachments. Apathy is effortless. Those who align against our beliefs, who challenge our traditions and societal standards, are dedicated and robust with their demands.

Our beliefs require protection and that same degree of effort. Can we afford to shy away from the fact that homosexuality is wrong? Since our silence offers the opportunity for misdirected messaging, our message must be heard. It's wrong in the Bible, it's incompatible with society's most important and necessary calling and it will become a gate opener for additional anti-societal and immoral practices.

Right is right and wrong is still wrong. Homosexuality is a wrong and immoral dead end. We need to recognize that while the current battle rages around the sanctity of marriage, the war itself is against Christianity.

America's dominant Christian faith brought a serviceable moral clarity to a young Republic. Today, those pillars of faith and belief in God and Country are being challenged. Our voices must sing with praise and adoration for the revered and solemn state of marriage. And marriage, throughout time, has and always will consist of one man and one woman.

Winning at What Price?

April 15, 2013

There was a time when the Chairman or a leading spokesman for Augusta National would precede the TV viewing of each year's Masters Tournament with a message of assurance that it was their intent to limit the airing of commercials to just three minutes per hour. This was especially anticipated and appreciated during the final two rounds since Thursday and Friday's coverage is provided by that talk-a-thon sports channel ESPN. However, this reassurance was absent from this year's ABC coverage. So, it's with deep regret that the most rigid of traditional institutions has relinquished their once-a-year pinnacle of classy showmanship. And it is with deeper regret that this format change pales in comparison to the ensuing drama which may stain this hallowed institution.

Parallel with TV's growth and improved viewing, Augusta National Golf Club's Masters Tournament has become somewhat of an American tradition, which for many signals the arrival of spring. Its magnolia lined entrance provides viewers and players alike with the expectations of a panorama filled with a bevy of dogwood/azalea/magnolia beauty, which tends to announce the end of winter. Not only has The Masters retained its original tournament identity without bowing to a particular corporate sponsor, over the years, The Masters has also enforced a strict attendance decorum for acceptable conduct which other golfing venues currently lack.

All this said and for the millions of viewers who look forward to this premier golfing event, the master's has endured in both its finery and traditions—that is, until Friday's round.

On Masters Sunday, golfing enthusiasts were all well aware of Tiger's error on the fifteenth hole during the second round. To Tiger's credit, he honestly related his actions and intentions leading to his faux pas. Apparently, in his mind, his actions were without fault as he routinely submitted his score from that day's round.

However, this is the rub. A player is expected to be well versed with the USGA's rulebook. Since this is their chosen profession and the major source of their economic well-being, this familiarization with one's work rules becomes inherent, or at least compatible, with one's overall expectations for success. So, ignorance of the rules is no excuse.

As to this particular USGA violation, this is not of the freakish nature when kneeling on one's towel is translated by the USGA as a technique for improving one's lie. No sir, the scenario leading to this error is a common occurrence for both the professional and the weekend hacker. Who has not had to "take a drop" when their ball becomes unplayable?

So, what transpired is not a rare situation but one of a common predicament. Of all the rules that the USGA detail and enforce, a professional should be well aware of the rules when "taking a drop." So, with this in mind, and owing to the fact that we are all human and mistakes or lapses do happen, it behooves that "august" (excuse the play on words) Augusta Rules Committee to be even more aware of any such infraction, especially one so common.

I am not privy to the ongoing reviews of tournament golf. However, the mere fact that there are so many infinitesimal rules to such minutely and ever-changing game situations, one would think that the number one player in the world's play would be under a guardian type view and/or review, especially when a penalty occurs. To base the Rules Committee's reaction upon an after-round interview in which Tiger confesses culpability; and for that same Rules Committee to delay their actions till the following morning is antithetical or at least neglectful to their general purpose.

I say this since these actions appear to ignore the fact that Tiger, which is the routine for all players, had in the interim, signed and turned in his inaccurate scorecard. Whether he knew it or not, this is USGA grounds for dismissal. Again, ignorance is no excuse with regards to the USGA. And with regards to that "august" Rules Committee, this fact was apparently deemed to be inconsequential, when in reality, it is the most consequential of his actions. Odd that compounding the original infraction with an improper scorecard would be ignored while the Committee thought best in waiting till the following day to meet with Tiger.

Golf is a game played by gentlemen. There are scores of instances when an infraction of the rules, which went unnoticed, were reported by the golfer himself. One such example even involved Mr. Bobby Jones. Golf's honesty along with the integrity of the game itself has always been its cornerstone and is especially evident and expected during the Masters.

In accordance with this hallowed tradition of integrity and gentlemanly honor, Tiger Woods' fame would have soared if he had followed Mr. Jones' example of sportsmanship. However, alluding to a recent rule's change, Tiger felt that he was abiding by the rules of the game. Even if technically correct, certainly shallow and self-serving since his opportunity to showcase his integrity and respect for the game lost out to his personal strive for golfing greatness.

The stated new rule, supposedly to benefit and protect golfers, in itself detours from the original purpose of rules defining the game. The rule states, "A penalty of disqualification may in exceptional individual cases be waived, modified or imposed if the Committee considers such action warranted. Any penalty less than disqualification must not be waived or modified. If a committee considers that a player is guilty of a serious breach of etiquette, it may impose a penalty of disqualification under this Rule."

The opening sentence releases the floodgates to endless interpretation and confusion. Rules are rules much in the same way that the law is the law. Given the facts in this case, the original infraction led to Tiger's disqualifying act when he knowingly or unknowingly submitted an improper scorecard. This is an open and shut violation and was previously treated as such. Granting Tiger's third round play not only stained his possible winning but committed immeasurable harm to the game of golf and to the historical traditions of which Bobby Jones intended that his Augusta course would preserve.

While flatly in denial of granting the number one golfer and crowd pleaser special treatment, the final determination was more forgiving than was the treatment of a fourteen-year-old from China. And I might add that the youngster displayed the class and integrity for which Bobby Jones' Masters is meant to promote. Guan Tianlang, without the normal benefit of being warned for slow play, accepted his one stroke penalty saying, "I respect the decision they make. They should do it because it's fair to everyone." His father remarked, ironically, "A rule is a rule."

If history provides clues, preferential treatment has surfaced in the past. I can remember when officials deemed an obstruction to be a "moveable object," thereby saving Tiger a one stroke penalty. The only problem was that it required over a dozen young male spectators to remove that "moveable object."

In another previous instance, a frustrated Tiger angrily swiped off his putter which produced a lengthy rip to the green he had just finished putting on. Little was said about the absence of assessing a USGA penalty, fine or worse.

Say whatever may be said about these unfortunate events, and whether once again, Tiger received special treatment, but few will deny that Tiger has energized the game's revenue and rewards. He is more of a walking corporation than he is an ordinary run of the mill professional golfer. TV tournament ratings dip when he is not playing and his five-year hiatus from winning a major has squeezed his career chances for besting Nicklaus' major record. With this Masters ruling, his chase remained, TV ratings were up and so was the increase in revenues.

In conclusion, the adage, "money talks and BS walks" tilts the question in favor of a blind eye. The fact that he did get away with the unthinkable of signing an incorrect scorecard, versus those of lesser fame and talent feeling the USGA's rigid sting, sort of closes the deal.

However, this is all history. The blemish has been recorded as Augusta did to itself what eluded Martha Burke; to break Augusta

National's invincibility. Left whispering through Augusta's dogwoods were those words from Guan Tianlang's father, "a rule is a rule." However, those dogwoods remain far removed from the confines of the Butler Cabin.

A Proud Message

July 5, 2013

My college roommate from 1962 asked my lady Carol and I to join him and his wife on a trip to Parris Island, S.C. to celebrate his grandson's "boot camp" graduation. Since I have been "Uncle Jim" to all their children and grandchildren for forever my acceptance was assured. Although Carol's brother had been a Major in the U.S. Army Special Forces, she had never been to a military installation. I, being a drafted Army vet, certainly never set foot on a Marine base, nor did I ever have any intention to. However, our two-day jaunt was the most inspiring and uplifting experience since that shock of our second 9/11.

That's right, our second. Someone should inform our media that America's first "9/11" was General Washington's defeat at The Battle of Brandywine, September 11, 1777.

As we all are inundated daily with levels of anti-Americanism, I thought it would be worthwhile to inform freedom loving Americans that, yes, freedom rings and it particularly rings loud and proud at Parris Island.

My friend's grandson walked the walk of so many who become transformed by our Nation's military. I saw it during my time in the Army and certainly, the Marines are famous for their version of "tough love." However, this was the first time I was so up front and personal with Corps traditions.

Every red-blooded American should have witnessed the graduation ceremony. There, in front of all family and friends were our best and our brightest but more importantly, those that take their sworn oath seriously enough to willingly put everything on the line. We would do well to demand that same level of oath loyalty from those elected!

What was evident throughout our visit was the pride, their personal manners and the respect which transcended through the military bearing of every passing Marine. Ironically, and intrinsic to this current attempt at curtailing the Christian influence within our military community, it must be acknowledged that our particular Marine casually mentioned that during his time in boot camp, he "found" religion.

In a setting that trains for the grittiest of war's essentials, Spirituality beckons an instinctual path for the inner peace and conviction which balances the average recruit's training. It also continues what was in place during Washington's uphill fight for our Independence. Devine intervention was often credited for turning uncertain times into favorable outcomes.

As the platoons marched into the enclosure, a Marine Corps band was in full throttle. As I previously mentioned, every American, especially the young, all would benefit by witnessing such a ceremony. There wasn't a dry eye in the place. The crispness of movement, the sword carrying Drill Instructors along with "the Colors" displayed transformed everyone in attendance to another American time. Our hearts were thumping with pride and patriotism. It was impossible not to be so affected.

Afterwards, every Marine was surrounded by family and friends for an endless amount of picture taking along with hugs, kisses and tears. These young men and women transmitted a measure of reassurance for our future with a knowledge that America was in good hands.

During lunch at a nearby restaurant, our Marine recounted the more intimate day to day details of Marine boot camp. One immediately sensed his pride, his self-confidence and his dedication. What this young man achieved was a far cry from what he had left behind. It was his turnaround, his awakening.

Throughout our Parris Island visit, one couldn't help but compare the average private's devotion verses the career politician's empty answers. Veterans who become our elected public servants share a differing perspective based upon their military experiences. Their sacrifices, whether it be during war or peacetime remain instilled and guide them to a more loyal and accountable performance. If only judged by one criterion, their sworn oath, this proven asset would be an immense benefit to all levels of governing.

So, in this time of American angst, of leadership which denies more than it promotes, let us all sleep more soundly in the knowledge that America is served well by her young men and women who wear her uniforms.

We should naturally salute the men and women in all the branches of the United States military since the values they learn while serving will benefit society in later years. This was so following our War for Independence as veterans laid down their arms to embark upon their legislative journeys. Today, it is again crucial since only the military remains as a fountainhead for basic American principles.

Appropriately, graduation took place on the eve of America's Day of Independence. At Parris Island, American pride was on display. Our society would do well to emulate that spirit; that Bulldog tenacity mixed with Spiritual guidance. Such a guiding source, contrary to Obama's claim, is present and everlasting. Just ask any Marine!

Missing the Mark

December 13, 2013

I swear, being an average American can often bring unbiased approaches when stirred generously with some useful common sense. I mean, what's with this "cure all" associated with a constitutional convention being held at the State level? Excuse me but whether it be at the State or Federal levels, politicians are still politicians. Or to put it in simpler terms, how many State budgets run in the red? These are the bumpkins who supposedly will act as our cavalry to the rescue?

Please do not take the wrong approach and credit me with a dislike of one TV talker who authored a book about this saving grace. In fact, I am a devout fan of his show and remain in awe of both his life's accomplishments and his Constitutional wisdom. However, at some point I believe that our Forefathers assigned, "we the people" to be the final arbitrators of our destiny. Paid spokesmen, whether honorable or otherwise, are just that, paid but with a degree of unknown integrity. I remain leery of trusting such a crucial setting to those who have yet to "come through in the clutch."

Also, we are in this current predicament by our own choosing. By that I mean that for too long, too many have for one reason or another, been too busy or have chosen indifference versus the goings on in far-off state capitols and in Washington. How many have said or heard said, "What difference does one vote make?" Or how about the ageless and defeatist chant of "you can't fight city hall."

During that same time span, good, hard working and patriotic Americans have believed in the rationalized assurances that, "it can't happen here in America." Inconceivably, as each passing election dashes our trust, we still manage to pick up our marbles and proceed as if all will somehow be resolved one day.

These prevailing twentieth century attitudes did not go unnoticed. For the most part, those elected became more opportunistic simply based upon our disinterest and our apathy. Together with their gift for speechifying, voters seemed to accept their oratory which defied common sense.

Not until the emergence of our Tea Party voice, have our highly paid weasels taken notice of those back home. For decades, individual fiefdoms, within this unauthorized bureaucracy, have been established and have flourished with a sort of give-and-take arrangement between these political entities. The eye opening 2010 election results, from the Republican "red wave" in Congress, turned the heads of many political grifters. They instinctively reasoned, and rightly so, that forces are at hand which could damage, or at least reveal, their systematic thievery.

Identifying what takes place in Washington as being the epitome of corruption simply tap dances around the costly and infectious system which we have refused to address. We have a habit of finger-pointing without any follow up—that is, until 2010.

We would be foolish to assume that what ails Washington remains limited or particular to our insatiable federal bureaucracy. State and local officials are not immune and, in many cases, jump in greedily. Some earn qualifying stripes; a silent approval that if selected or politically endorsed to the next level, the status quo will remain unfettered since the newcomer has previously been tested.

Is there any wonder as to the degree of vitriol that leading spokespersons from both parties now direct at the Tea Party in general and its elected representatives in particular? Members of the establishment have witnessed firsthand the threats from the proposed agenda of limited governing, which current and future Tea Party representation will continue endorsing. As such, the recent rancor exhibited by Boehner and his associates is to be sadly expected. Echoing today's slanting of media coverage, is the most condemning identity heard within the halls of congress; that of being a Constitutionalist or a radical Tea Party supporter.

So it is that the only players who retain a vested interest to preserve our Constitution and to continue cleaning house are the ones paying the bills, those who are getting raked over the coals. It is again, and always will be, "we the people."

Handing over the possible convergence of a Constitutional convention onto a lower level of governing is akin to replacing the lion in the chicken coop with an ally cat. The menu, or in this case, the policies, will never change. The only difference, in all probability, is with the amount and at which level the corruption will best fit.

The Duck Dynasty Threat

December 20, 2013

When it is deemed that one may be out of sorts with the supposed mainstream thought while gaining stature to the point of public respect and admiration, it seems that an interviewing hound dog will be sent sniffing at the trail.

Who remembers the popular baseball pitcher, John Rocker? Back in his day, I personally bought a T shirt with "Rocker for President" on it. Remember his literary ambush? While it worked then, the difference today is that not only does Phil Robertson obviously walk the walk on his weekly TV show, Duck Dynasty, his lifestyle rekindles our lost spark of Americanism. Gee, I think I just stumbled upon what caused such an indignant response.

The immediateness of A&E's compliance to the outspoken demands from the LGBT quarter bares their hidden desire to extinguish what they created. This logic applies when the overall texture of the entertainment industry is reviewed. Given that this industry represents an influential extension to our liberal media behemoth, is there any wonder as to why such popularity for tradition must be squashed?

The behind-the-scenes collaboration which took place prior to Robertson's GQ interview appears to be an almost certain fact. And given the outspoken and honest dossier of the subject at hand, attaining the desired result would be a snap. And certainly, it was, given the man's honesty.

Anyone who doubts such shenanigans still believes that Peter Pan is aloft in the clouds. Get real. Look at what the wildly popular Duck

Dynasty show has produced! Today, with Christmas buying nearing its peak, consider the "Duck" merchandise and memorabilia that is selling off the shelves. Check out Phil Robertson's "Happy, Happy, Happy" book sales. Even Uncle Si's work is a hit. Get real, this was and culminated into exactly what wasn't drawn up or expected. So, take down the head and the rest will follow!

Who can argue that Duck Dynasty stands apart in the entertainment field? And why? Because it represents what has been so fervently devalued during this last half of a century. Not one single industry "head" could have expected such a responsive following and for one very obvious reason. All the American bases had been previously covered.

Think about it folks, what has taken place during this period that has not devalued our standards, our expectations, our self-image and most critically, our country's independence? Do we need to replay or itemize all that has been discarded during these fifty plus years? Let's start with our emphasis upon a new age understanding, a desensitization of Americanism, our heightened awareness for equality, the need for global inclusiveness, the rise of global rather than national identity (ala global brotherhood) and of course this touchy feely politically correct mantra. Given this line up, can we begin to see why this GQ interview grew into such a necessity?

Whatever was the reason, A&E had already reaped the "bennies" from the presentation of a show which highlighted what is basically America. Very possibly, it was a typical act of "salting the wound" in that "corporate" had previously written the public's American epitaph. The ability for America's reclamation was determined to be nil. So, this presentation actually reflected back upon that "corporate" mentality which viewed America with disgust and disfavor. Essentially, it was their "in house" pat on the back.

Within their disconnect from real American life, whether it be lost in the swamp waters of Louisiana, the pine thickets of the Carolinas or the mountains of Pennsylvania; the gist of our American breed was ignored. Their elitist perspectives saw this as a done deal, one that called for a self-congratulatory triumph. However, once publicly uncorked, the "Duck" genie flew out of the bottle and the countryside responded.

This deserves some thought since it mostly likely lies somewhere between a very possible possibility and that of being actual. It does make sense in that the flow explains from start to finish what took both the country and those A&E executives by surprise.

Consider the magnitude of it all. It would be one thing if this was relegated to those in the "redneck" Southern States. However, its appeal, showcased by its dedicated following, intermingles throughout our great land. In a word, it unites! And that in itself is enough reason to vilify an honorable American father who loves God and country!

It Is What It Is, Or Is It?

January 8, 2014

Ask yourself a question. How is it that from time to time, Americans adopt catchy new phrases in true monkey see monkey do fashion? Can anyone tell me what "have a good one" actually means? Have a good what! Without getting into the muck, there's a bevy of possibilities! Certainly, this transition from "have a good day" cannot be rooted in academia, or do I overrate the so-called achievements of higher learning?

Consider this deep-thinking title. Certainly, what is, will always be just that. So why, in so many postgame interviews, football players add this insulting "it is what it is" when condensing game results or even with future contract negotiations. Why? Are we all robots with the same predictable verbal replies, akin to what Pavlov instilled into his dogs? What caused our acceptance for being this bunch of nameless munchkins, or if you must, "dudes."

And what of this "dude" identity? Are our birth names now so antiquated and confusing? If we all are now nameless jumbles, without differing identities, what of the female "dude?" Is she a "dudette" or in this era of unisex conformity, are our young ladies nameless or could it be that they fortunately retain their given birth names?

From a self-appraisal aspect, are these previous paragraphs sufficiently antagonizing enough so that we might question this brainless mimicking? Or is it that these questions are simply the ageless musings from stuffy old men? Hopefully, the ease of dismissing the uncomfortable will be ignored so that we may take stock in what has crept onto our American turf.

Second thought, these new age quips actually do seem to mesh with what has evolved educationally. Just how can our youth properly learn, so that they may be "better equipped to deal" with the changing demands of our modern computerized society if one cannot even spell correctly? Certainly, various TV advertisements and roadside billboards contribute to our youth's learning dysfunctions.

Couple this lazy spelling venue with Common Core's dismissal of teaching the cursive skill of handwriting. Just what remains in today's curriculum? Already, pocket calculators have eliminated the learning of math tables. History was long ago diluted into "social studies." Yet, more and more revenue is demanded for the unconstitutional Department of "Education."

Do we get a sense that something is amiss? The generations which will fill our shoes have been marginalized before even knowing how to drive. And if we as adults are any indicators, they will be as eager with conformity as we were with these stupid little quips.

This transition, from our most basic of identities and timeless functions is frightening when considering its common usage and daily needs. The inherent individuality from our individual birth names of John or Mary, Tom or Barbra has been trashed in preference for this bland and indistinguishable moniker of "dude."

Such large-scale change didn't come about by happenstance or from a natural passing. In all likelihood, the unprincipled and morally bankrupted Hollywood, in conjunction with those wisdom spigots known as professors got together and then did a speed dial to all their corporate chieftains and politico brethren so as to further befuddle an aimless citizenry.

At some point, change for the sake of change becomes tiresome and insulting. This is the case with this universal claim of "Dude." Forgive my backward glance but my parents chose my name at birth and by that name I like to think I've conducted myself based upon my family reputation, our recognition and trust of one another, respect and a regard not to embarrass those I love. This "Dude alias lacks such conditions which is par for the course since basically, it's just a PC term for "Hey you!"

An Applicable Comparison

January 31, 2014

I fed and housed my boxers for over forty years. During that time, I never once witnessed a hesitation with regards to their loyalty. They were my pets and we loved each other. It was a balanced and wonderful time which always brought great joy.

I make mention of man's best friend simply in contrast to what I continue to feed and house. That would be the members from all levels of government. Needless to say, these returns, if any, are not comparable.

Oh yes, another similarity just came to mind. Boxers are a breed which has insatiable appetites. Contrary to smaller varieties, the food in the dish, no matter the amount will be eaten in total. Cutesy breeds, such as toy poodles and the like, will eat limited amounts and walk away from a half full bowl. My "pups" always looked for more after emptying their bowl. Sadly, but too often, this is a common trait with those that I feed and house in government. Always, they search for more.

At the outset, the association with dogs and politicians is diverse since "owning" a pup is a voluntary and individual decision. A politician's is a necessary agent representing a "necessary evil." My boxers are not evil, not even necessary to those living without such companionship. And while I prefer one breed, my choosing is my choosing, not by an engineered choice from glib career lips and slanted news reports! Thusly, our usual let downs and disappointments from lofty campaign oratories are of our own making, as is our delightful rewards from our reliable friends!

Also relevant between these two worlds are our nagging thoughts for term limits versus just the opposite with our four-legged buddies! Near the end, we all pin our hopes upon the family vet who we believe, during our final visit, will somehow find a miraculous cure.

So, can we all agree that dogs of any breed are more enjoyable, loyal, and ever so more giving than that of a stale politician who, after a lengthy career, still treats you as a stranger?

Another difference which acts as a political insurance policy is that in society, governments must be created so that limitations and societal rules can be instituted to ensure its peaceful perpetuity.

This is not the case when opting for a man's best friend. Despite the campaign rhetoric, which at election time would beset the voter into thinking in a like manner, the normal bloviating politico is anything but a "best friend." In fact, given the current situation and the agenda which now comes from both sides of the aisle, it would not be a stretch to think of government's role as that of being an unwanted nighttime intruder!

Through this differing perspective, our insanity shines through. Our house pet, at times our guardian, is a willing expense which more than rewards with undying loyalty, reliability and love. But what, on the other hand, do we get when our association and reliance is tied to a politician? So why do we continue to display such sturdy belief over and over again when the results, in lieu of all the alibis and excuses, remain the same?

This failing format takes on an aura of control, dependency and even a touch of sick behavior. As it is difficult to justify, at the very least, it reveals how little effort there is prior to redoing our same mistakes.

In Pennsylvania, Arlen Specter continued as the State's Senate representative for decades. Oops, one moment please. States are without official representation in Washington since the Seventeenth Amendment. Formerly, Senators were chosen by their particular State's legislators. They were considered and originally designed to be Ambassadors of State.

But I digress. Specter, like many others, was re-elected time and time again based upon his conservative vent. The only problem was his vent was anything but! Has there ever been a dog owner who keeps giving treats to his puppy time and time again after the dog does his business on the floor? This is the sad reality with today's voters!

America's Daffy Sunset

February 25, 2014

Who can now still question this unrelenting scheme which has been targeting American principles, heritage and traditions, especially when it now involves two American rocks; that being the Father of our Country, George Washington and America's beloved screen hero, John Wayne? During the last few days, this is exactly what took place and while this insult came to light in the sleepy hollow of Daytona Beach, it never-the-less is indicative of a much broader policy against American values and sacred beliefs nationwide.

How many American readers look forward to their local paper's "This Day in History" section every morning? It provides an interesting and non-political respite before reading the dreadful news of natural or man-made disasters or Obama's latest illegal power grab. Well, last Friday, on February 22nd, even that enjoyable brevity was withheld.

Here in Daytona Beach, our local tabloid saw fit to begin my morning by its omission of President George Washington's birthday. For me and I suspect many other Americans, this insult is unimaginable. Directly under "This Day in History" column is a listing of "Birthdays" of well-known Americans. Briefly detailed were six recognizable names along with their ages. Again, President Washington didn't qualify while that instigator of political intrigue, David Axelrod's fifty-ninth was noted.

Before proceeding, I might add that at the bottom of "this Day in History," it was noted and very much appreciated that the "Miracle on Ice" took place in Lake Placid, N.Y." Certainly, a fitting day to recognize another underdog triumph.

On the following morning, this masquerade of proper journalism saw fit to publish an entire page devoted to the subject of, "Manhood in America." Centered at the top was a picture of the Duke, John Wayne; all decked out in his western finery, astride a horse of smallish stature in comparison.

Under Mr. Wayne's picture was the past tense caption, "No Question What It Meant to be a Man in America." It was followed by this brief explanation under the picture; "it was typified by Gary Cooper, above, and John Wayne on the movie screen, by the GIs on America's foreign battle fields, by the executives with homemaker wives and no corporate worries about gender diversity."

For those of my generation, not only are the acting styles and the characters portrayed by Cooper and Wayne distinct, especially in Wayne's case, but AP writer David Crary is apparently clueless as to who was featured on horseback. For us balding or white-haired readers, Crary's "Gary Cooper, above," either attempts to mislead the young or in fact illustrates his own ignorance of our Western movie icons.

The original intent of our "free press" was to truthfully inform Americans. Today, that pursuit has become blurred if not perverted. Now, the goal is to influence and persuade opinion through its anti-American bias. How else to explain Crary's insipid presentation of "what it meant to be a man in America"

His mistaking of Wayne with Cooper might be innocent but his take on the "…executive with homemaker wives…" leaves little wiggle room. Also, when one entertains his …"no corporate worries about gender diversity," it's easy to translate his progressive agenda.

Is this what morning papers are all about? The "Manhood in America" article included the by-line, "Bit by bit, macho stereotypes lose ground." Crary's celebratory theme is hard to ignore.

Also consider his subheading, "A Variety of Thoughts on the Subject." Under this category, Ann Friedman, whoever she may be, offered; "Ultimately, confusion about modern masculinity is a good thing: It means we're working past the outmoded definition." Are we supposed to believe that "manhood" is now passé? Or is manhood a useful but shelved pantry item, only to be used in cases of extreme emergencies; maybe something akin to a fire extinguisher?

Or how about this feminist take: "The women's movement showed that women didn't want to be restricted by their gender role, and it's opened things up for men to not be restricted as well - they can be stay-at-home dads, they can be nurses." To that I would respond that I don't know about Crary's experiences, but men have been and continue to be the greatest of nurses when one yells "medic" or "corpsman!"

Am I being too harsh on Mr. Crary's piece? After all, he did open with his take on how the American male was formerly measured; "the stoic hero...vanquished all foes and offered women a muscular shoulder to cry on." However, this was immediately marginalized with his, "but that was before feminism, gay-rights activism, and metrosexuals." Would it be rude to inquire as to just what is a "metrosexual? Are they also allowed to marry?

Seriously, after sixty-nine years, I never knew how involved and differentiating being a male could be. After all, walking to school with a bag of marbles and a pocketknife in my trousers was "every day.". And as Crary likes his before/after transition, I didn't crave to know my inner self or question my masculine role. I just wanted to shoot marbles at recess and if a fight broke out, well, we were all friends again afterwards. Funny, we all survived without this new age need for counseling.

It's amazing that my generation made it into adulthood without the guidance from say a James O'Neil, who as a psychology professor at the University of Connecticut offered his own wisdom with, "There's denial about men having problems related to gender roles. We need to break through that."

Are you kiddin' me? Is this garbage in, garbage out or what? In this era of scare employment, uncontrollable authority, sagging morals and now men, who for whatever reason, find it gratifying or more fulfilling when being in touch with their gentler side, what has or will remain sacred? Is there nothing that these social engineers can't screw up?

If we judge this evolving American landscape through the prism of women in combat roles while their touchy-feely hubbies choose the perfect apron to wear while preparing dinner, understanding for what makes Putin so cheerful comes into a clearer focus.

Ironically, if Putin was asked one question, it would be our adversary who could provide a clear analysis of Crary's piece. Which America would he prefer? Would it be the rugged individualism of John Wayne or this new age "modern masculinity" of Brokeback Mountain? Putin's choice would be obvious and so must be ours, since this answer will mold America's future and her traditional John Wayne like men!

Intentional Media Fiction

May 24, 2014

After a self-imposed break, I'm back to inform that it's just not the Philadelphia readers who are confronted with syndicated writer Dick Polman's Constitutional ignorance. It seems that my local paper has fallen under his uninformed spell also.

My morning coffee was greeted with Polman's bearded grin and accompanying article entitled, "Gridlock forces president's hand." From my limited understanding of the world of journalism, I believe that each individual paper pens the headline. However, its origins are of no consequence since both the headline and the content of Polman's essay amount to an inaccurate interpretation of a President's authority.

Polman writes and concurs that "Obama's only choice was to circumvent the legislative stalemate…" The writer, in effect, endorses our current President's penchant for issuing Executive Orders at will, unopposed and unlimited in scope and authority.

Although the legality of an Executive Order is acknowledged, what isn't permitted is its application outside of the Executive branch. Modern day Presidents have ridden this restraint into the ground. While it is often defended with the selected quip, "Washington wrote Executive orders too," what is not mentioned, for obvious reasons, is that our first President limited his, as it was designed, to within the Executive branch.

For too long, what the average American is being inundated with are the perverse and intentionally incorrect readings and interpretations of our Constitution, with special usurpations upon its parameters of governmental restraints and limitations. Such positions seem in lockstep with lawless administrations.

Polman's essay is just the latest in a saturation agenda which eventually takes hold over a majority of citizens who have never been exposed to, let alone taught in detail, the particulars of Constitutional governing.

This system of selective, slanted or just blatantly false news reporting forms the definition of a liberally biased media. It is impossible, from a daily perspective, not to become swayed and/or influenced by this system of intentional misinformation. Polman's article provides the perfect example.

Our government is made up of three separate and defined branches, each being watchful over the others. So, just how is it that a President can, as Mr. Polman assumes, "circumvent" the Legislative branch with his issuance of an executive order? If this is the case, then what benefit, or reason is it for Congress to exist? And, if that be the reasoning and eventuality, just what has happened to our Constitution or to its three branches of separate governmental operations?

Polman's essay stands as a monument to not only its degree of blatant absurdity, but more importantly, to the expectations that it will be considered and eventually believed. This may sound "conspiratorial" but open your hearts and minds to consider just where in our written laws is the word "democracy?" Yet today, politicians and voters alike believe in this absurdity. The same can be said for the "separation of church and state."

These are the end results of repetitive messaging from people in seemingly high places. Influence soaks downward like water. Without realizing, the words of a national writer become more credible than say, the words I am writing. But their prestige is assumed while truth remains firm.

A perfect example is the recent coverage of the Nevada rancher, Cliven Bundy, as the public learned of his "freeloading" on land not owned, while his cattle threatened the endangered tortoise. All distortions.

Without detailing the many sordid reports, how many have heard of the arrangement of co-ownership, or to be more precise, the "split estate" for land use? How many have been informed as to the abuse of governmental ownership, in terms of total acreage, of all our western states? Or of the split estate's arrangement of surface and sub surface rights? All these facts have been omitted from the endless reporting on radio, TV and in print for a reason. Yet all are pertinent to what took place.

One other instance of running roughshod over our Constitutional law was attached to a local headline declaring a Pennsylvania first; "Gay couples begin to marry in Pa." It's been reported that six couples filed a lawsuit to block South Dakota's gay marriage ban.

Within this AP report, the anticipation for its success flows with every word. However, these couples have managed to hire counsel for arguing against the legitimacy of a law which was duly passed in that State's legislature and was signed by the Governor in 1996. In addition, it was further enforced by a 2006 voter-approved constitutional amendment.

These examples typify the misinformation being presented to a well-meaning and trusting citizenry. However, this off-course direction seems purposeful and intentional. With the end result being the abolishment of American absolutes, just what will remain? What is the law if it isn't rigidly enforced and respected? Do our emotions and wants to overrule and if so, what will tomorrow offer?

West Point Still Stands

May 30, 2014

The President was here yesterday, at West Point, our Nation's most historic military institution, speechifying at a graduation which at any other time would both salute the graduate's military commissions and honor their solemn pledge of "Duty, Honor, Country."

This is not an ordinary college graduation to be sure. Those in uniform chose their uniform rather than the civilian tradition of cap and gown. To be precise, they have been trained for leadership roles in the art of war. Their entire being and future is on the line and this they readily accept. As such, I believe this commencement was their first test at being an "officer and a gentleman," as they all had to endure Obama's dribble."

So, "enter stage left," the "commander-in-chief" shucks and jives across the stage to the podium. Immediately, the lack of a military bearing sets the stage for what is to come. And in true Obama fashion, he doesn't disappoint!

Without recounting the political references of blame, the insults or the "me, me, me" utterances, the President conferred upon the 2014 edition of The Long Grey Line the assurance that they would be the first class to graduate since 9/11 that didn't have to worry about an Afghanistan deployment. Needless to say, this Presidential ignorance requires the proper perspective, given the subsequent lackluster cadet response.

Do we recall attending one of those cap and gown graduations at a State Teacher's College, back when such institutions were still an economic advantage? How many would applaud that hypothetical commencement speaker when assuring the graduates that, "don't worry, yours is the first class since 9/11 that won't have to enter the teaching field."

Now obviously, Obama is away from his handpicked and adoring audiences. So, what to do? Let's insult, degrade and minimize their devotion, loyalty and possible sacrifice. Obama is talking to a class which has not only excelled academically; they have undergone rigorous military training. Here sits the Army's future mud eating platoon leaders and company commanders and eventually, our future field grade officers. How do they start their military careers? Well, they have to sit and listen to a commander-in-chief who has yet to prove his citizenship, who heads an administration which employs the tenacious IRS against his political opponents; but more importantly, at every turn, has shown his disfavor of our American military.

The cadets, more than the average citizen, remember Obama's questionable dereliction of duty, from his unknown whereabouts, during the night of those Benghazi attacks, which after two years, the White House has yet to explain Obama's whereabouts. This remembrance is a hard pill for West Pointers to swallow.

Yesterday's speech is just another insulting example of the anti-Americanism which flows through this man's veins. And it is his record which proves this repeatedly. In addition to his West Point words, Obama's record as President is a well-worn horror flick.

However, his days are numbered, my personal count stands as of the 29th is at 967. As these numbers continue to dwindle, his tenacious need for lawless decrees will no doubt increase.

Yesterday, he preached to the cadets that "the world is changing," and that it is their "task to respond to this new world." This is hardly a news flash since change has been constant since the end of WWII. However, his references to a changing world and "this new world" seemed inconsistent when preceding his selection from George Washington's 1796 Farewell Address. In part, Obama quoted, "...Tis our true policy to steer clear of permanent Alliances with any portion of the foreign world."

Contrary to the advice from our Father of our Country, who happens to be the only President who turned down an offer of a kingship, Obama sternly and stiff lipped contradicted President Washington with his, "We don't have a choice to ignore what happens beyond our borders." Of course, such bravado is the bequest of an arm chaired "commander-in-chief," rather than the mounted Washington leading from in front of his Army.

One last critique of Obama's oratory epitomizes his American disloyalty with his support for the UN's Law of the Sea Treaty. Given that most Americans remain uninformed, suffice to say that it is a totally anti-American pact which restricts usage of the world's waterways to the point of limiting our Naval comings and goings. And this particular policy position is what he decided to include at a West Point graduation?

At this point, Obama's narcissistic nature is tugging at his looming relinquishment of the Presidency. Whether it be his lavishly styled vacations or his wielding of his infamous pen/phone decrees, coming down to earth for this imposter should be a welcome relief for us all, especially so for those uniformed attendees.

Acknowledgement and Thanks

June 28, 2014

To all the aging Vietnam veterans out there, it appears that a reversal is beginning to unfold, saluting our long-ago service and sacrifice. Aside from those "welcome home" parades of the late eighties, this is an individual and spontaneous effort from passersby and strangers. Its impromptu one-on-one exchange is an honest outpouring devoid of any fanfare. And equally important, it is being received by a set of grateful ears.

It would be an injustice not to mention that for those who lived lives in the shadows of past victories and within earshot of the bellowing voices of protest, the Vietnam War's general conduct, its rules of engagement and its decision-making styles are sadly being replayed today. The ignored "lessons of Vietnam" burns equally in the hearts of veterans and sadly connects today with yesterday.

However, long overdue recognition of past sacrifice is surfacing within an age group which now shoulders our Nation's burdens. Again, and for too long, the current generation has been embroiled in another no-win situation. As each generation of veterans pass the torch of responsibility, so it is that we Vietnam vets salute our younger veterans for their service and sacrifice.

Today, the Vietnam veteran's proud claim is that returning veterans are appropriately welcomed. This now forms our legacy, a validation of our sacrifice and in part, has become a by-product from our own homecoming. We are thrilled and proud that today offers a supportive Nation to those most deserving.

I must apologize for my digression but this all ties into what I am now proud to admit. Based upon the comments of other vets, and in addition my own personal experience, there is an increasing nod of respect being shown to the Vietnam veteran. And it is generally being offered by those whose age brackets today's sacrifice.

In addition to our thinning white hair and/or grey beards, many strangers connect the dots to our hats and T shirts, along with our bumper stickers. In this regard, young Americans are increasingly offering their heartfelt thanks.

I might add that twice a year, my local community of Daytona Beach welcomes hundreds of thousands of Harley riders, many of whom fly their POW flags, in addition to their bike's assortment of military decals. Their unison of thunder and individualistic bearing screams of an Americanism which was proudly paid for and can never be tread upon.

Just recently, while walking up to a store front, a young man held open the door and waited for me to enter. Later, as I began my fueling at the pump, I heard someone bellow from a distance, "sir!" I looked around to see that same man trying to get my attention and then heard him thanking me for my service.

Now I must admit, at first, these well-wishers caught me by surprise for obvious reasons. We've been yelled at quite often in the past and hardly with the offering of Blessings. I am still caught off guard but darn if it isn't nice to finally hear.

A friend of a friend once asked me about my car's decal and the POW flag in the front of my house. He was indeed my senior and sort of chided me for not "getting over it." This line of thought is common, but I think my answer served his indifference.

I said that in part, that when I wear my hat or a T shirt, I do so out of pride and brotherhood. It's a way for one veteran to greet another who, without such recognition, would continue unrecognized. So now, we notice each other with handshakes and "welcome home" wishes. But equally important, wearing such is my way of making up for my own sense of disloyalty a long time ago.

When I returned, I immediately took off my Army uniform. Given the climate, it was easier than to proudly wear what was so gallantly earned by so many. The one time that I did wear my uniform was in respect to my mother's wishes to do so at church. So, unlike veterans of previous wars, I for one, and I imagine many of my brothers, took the easy way out. This is the type of memory which lasts and is why I and others, I assume, wear our pride "on our sleeves."

In closing, I'd just like to say welcome home to all my brothers and sisters who have borne the grittier side of our foreign adventures. And to those well-wishers, a big "thank you!" Also, please excuse our quizzical looks or expressions since this is a new experience. Just know that for the Vietnam veteran, we appreciate your respect and well wishes more than we could ever express.

The Wonder of It All

November 15, 2014

Lo and behold, our fascination with the educated have just come back to bite us. Since WWII, American parenting embraced the sentiment, "we want more for our kids," and by offering them a better life in that "we didn't want them to have to struggle like we did." With this approach, we began to spoil the child while throwing out the rod. Along the way, common sense and a useful reality of life from experience and struggle was sacrificed.

Embedded within this quest for success and ease of living was and still is the golden chalice of a college degree. This was theorized as the gateway, a piece of paper that would begin the journey to success and finery.

So basically, there began this notion that if one didn't graduate from college, one wouldn't achieve a large degree of success in life. I can personally recall this premise since it was prevalent during my youth. In reality, this beginning became a preference which would later produce an elitist culture. What was forged into the minds of the younger generations came full circle with Gruber's blunt assessments of the "average" American.

Now the wonder of it all is when Jonathan Gruber publicly espouses his elitist doctrines. Where did this thinking come from and how dare he say such things! Actually, Americans have been treated to the content of his college lecturing since these are the morsels which students must master when seeking high grades. As a result, it all makes sense when our returning college students dumbfounded us with their new aged theories during holiday and summer breaks.

College is not the real world nor is this "absent minded professor" preaches. However, college lecturers spread their words to a compulsory and often eager- to-excel audience. For a moment, imagine being transported into such a limited environment. Listening to such recognizable gibberish would be laughable, even intolerable, given our own life's experiences. However, imagine the young who lack the ability for such comparisons. What is that saying, and I'm paraphrasing, "as the twig is bent, so grows the tree?"

A useful rule of thumb equates to the more prestigious the degree from a certain college of university, higher is its elitism curve; or in a more practical sense, the richer the tuition, the more Grubers on staff.

This particular professor has, in one fell swoop, said goodbye to the campus for the whirlwind skullduggery of the political world, with its glistening monetary rewards. However, his assumed private lecturing circuit just became public knowledge. One might say that his brilliance is not so enlightening outside of his campus sanctuary. Coupled with that transition is his apparent cluelessness as to how the real world actually works.

What stands out with ironic humor is that Obama sought out advice from one with the same egotistical and/or narcissist nature as his own. Adoration and acclaim drives both yet Obama was blinded by his compelling need for completing America's emersion into his Socialist transformation.

As we are digesting Gruber's insulting theories, we should also realize the degree to which attaining success had been hammered home. He is hopeless, captured within this need to excel and as such, any and all tools leading to his success are fare game. He is without sensitivity or compassion in that his goal-oriented drive justifies any means.

As he has opened up his deceptive formulas to public ridicule, we should take this opportunity to realize that the vast majority of TV talking heads are of the same pedigree. Their commentary usually includes an elitist blend when expressing their tidbits. For a moment, consider just how much expertise can be had before reaching the age of forty.

So, Gruber is sadly the tip of a very disjointed segment of our citizenry. What makes him stand out from the rest is his brutal revelation while others seem more cautious of disturbing their audience. Rather they have chosen the more refined path with a more secure and settled future.

What is now needed is a systematic revamping of our educational system. While the college arena continues as a fortress subsidized in part by private funding, the realm of public education is deplorable; especially so, since learning now includes the ugly head of Islam. This must be our Clarion call!

If left untouched, our world being educated and ultimately led by thousands of little egotistical Grubers is bad enough without adding Sharia spice to the mix. The protection of our children should require a "no sacrifice too great" effort.

What Will Remain of America?

January 15, 2015

At what point will modern-day Americans wake the hell up? We have lazed around, enjoying our non-exertive creature comforts while those who are diligent in their agendas haven't missed a beat. At what point will we realize that it isn't "global awareness," "congenial compatibility" or as in this latest case, "religious pluralism." It's conquest and we are the damn targets!

These "politically correct" and asinine terms disguise the ongoing threat against our Country and our way of life. Make no mistake, we who live and enjoy the fruits of liberty are under attack as much as were those who perished in those 9/11 twin towers. It's just that at this stage of a minimal Muslim population percentage, it's more polished, compatible and persuasive than what will follow.

All one has to do is to look to France for an understanding of what is in store for America. Conversely, all one has to do is to look to Australia for an understanding of what needs to be done. Assimilate or leave!

France has permitted the encampments known as "no-go" zones, and in doing so, it seems that France can't get past being France. While we on the other side of the Atlantic have become distant finger pointers, or more to the fact, pointers with little or no "skin in the game," we also fail to realize that this will occur here if we continue with our appeasements.

The latest example of a suicidal America occurred at Duke University. Recent CNN headlines announced that, "Duke University's decision to sound Muslim call to prayer riles some," pretty much sums up this insanity.

This "top ten" rated American university reasoned that this "represents a larger commitment to religious pluralism that is at the heart of Duke's mission."

With this kind of perspective, what more needs to be said; especially when America previously expelled any possible connection with Christianity being taught or even mentioned in our elementary and secondary public school system.

Duke has been known as a Christian institution since its inception. What better platform for a Muslim infiltration effort? And make no mistake, it is infiltration and Duke's Christian heritage attracted this crusade.

What has happened to our resolve since our 9/11 attack? Probably the same as was the case prior to that fateful day. The majority of Americans viewed the subject of Vietnam as merely an historical reference, yet for those who served, we remember policies which devalued our sacrifice and eventually reversed our mission. Today's adversary is energized by these failures and this awareness is essential, for the need to know one's enemy is as old as war itself.

America may view reversing policies as being part and parcel of foreign trade-offs, but to our enemies, this encourages their ambitions. When religious fervor is added to their mix, forget logic, diplomacy or this insipid "religious pluralism." Their beliefs demand capitulation of the infidel. There is no middle ground and once attained, their rule will be ruinous and bloody. Their recent promotion of beheadings signals what lies in wait.

Today, we are a nation of well-meaning fools. We believe as we always have—that life is important, and that fairness is in every heart, especially at Duke University! Like I said, "Fools!"

We are facing what past nations faced and the picture remains the bloody same. Duke's dean, Christy Lohr Sapp's attitude that, "It connects the university to national trends in religious accommodation" is dangerous hogwash. Somebody had better inform Ms. Sapp that this threat of vicious domination is a real one and that her pluralistic views place all the students, along with our Country, in mortal danger.

The problem with America is that the vast majority of our citizens have not experienced sacrifice at any level. For too many decades, adults provided "a better life" for their children. In doing so, they have eliminated any of life's uncertainties, including sacrifice. This is a setting for which our enemies relish.

As for the beheaders, they consider it as a sign from Allah as to why the mighty armies of America cannot win at war. They view the leaving of 58,000 plus on the battlefield, then signing a peace agreement, as a sign of weakness and ultimately, representative of a vulnerable and unworthy opponent. While we glow over our WWII triumphs, our enemies concentrate upon the more relevant "what have you accomplished lately" aspects of our bravado.

Another advantage is their rigidity in religious beliefs. Any religion which touts the waiting of 72 virgins will have its immediate followers; however, what is America's belief, her drive? All they see is our disunity and disbelief. Is there any doubt as to what awaits?

Not to outdo the "no-go" zones of Europe but the "training camps" which have sprouted up throughout America foretells a more severe and lasting calamity. Are these already "no-go" camps? If so, their infiltration is further along than we all dare to admit.

This naïve approach of "religious pluralism" is the work of the protected, the guarded, those who are still free to spin and frolic within their preferred idealisms. They fail to understand the recruitment arena which they will be perpetrating. If this is allowed to continue, the college campus will join America's prison system as representing our enemy's most fertile recruitment centers.

For too long, many have rightly viewed our colleges and universities as havens for the proliferation of anti-American and socialistic doctrines. Now, Duke has opened the door for a blatant defiling of all that is American. What's next?

How Many Days Left?

February 5, 2015

The temporary resident of our American White House can suck on his bottom lip all he wants but the error of our ways will end in 715 days.

If nothing else, these two four years terms should be proof positive that whether it may be good looks, emotional oratory or a stylish swagger that may border on the jive, these and other feel-good motives will produce what America can ill afford.

During this time of National sacrifice, the absence of pro-American leadership defines a dereliction from duty. And judging by its lengthy duration and consistency, one would not be far off the mark in considering it rooted in the realm of treason.

While as a candidate who refused to wear the American flag lapel pin, for fear of taking sides or who didn't place his hand over his heart as our National anthem was being played may head the list chronologically, other discourtesies and questionable actions, such as bowing to a foreign head of State, or his recent "America isn't a Christian Nation" remark all contribute to a loyalty portfolio which stirs suspicion.

All of this, from his initial campaign to his re-election victory, originally came about from a rip-roaring emotional speech at the 2004 Democratic National Convention; a divisive oratory style which continues to appeal on and around the college circuit.

As with most street corner salesmen, the longer the oratory, the more likely is the overlap, the contradiction. When six plus years of non-performance is combined into the original premise, one begins to see not only how easily we were deceived but how shallow are the emotional tugs when devoid of any follow up.

As stated, Obama took off with his 2004 Convention address which highlighted America's social and governmental shortcomings. Included on his list were "a war with no end," "a dependence on oil," failing schools and paycheck shortcomings while working harder. Obama concluded that these problems were simply from "the absence of sound policies and sensible plans." The purpose of his remarks was to present the one who understood, who recognized and who would care enough.

But as with most sidewalk lawyers; their stumble comes from their excess chatter. In that same speech, Obama continued: The failure of leadership, the smallness of our politics, the ease with which we're distracted by the petty and trivial, our chronic avoidance of tough decisions, our preference for scoring cheap political points instead of rolling up our sleeves and building a working consensus to tackle big problems.

These, he reasoned, were contributing factors yet six years later, the same shortcomings not only remained, they represented his political ploys and steppingstones! While he may roll up his sleeves onstage, his toil ends when his mouth stops moving.

Now, on the other side of the ledger, and as our Forefathers charged, it is "we the people" who are the true sovereigns and as such are the most responsible for the government that we live under. As free people, our duty is to ensure that those who represent us are of noble and honest character, since the gavel of authority often succumbs to lesser mortals.

It is therefore vital that understanding and knowledge preclude our vote selection. In hindsight, we wonder as to "how could I have voted for him" yet at the time, we remember being too busy or "distracted by the petty or trivial" to spend a serious moment reading or really listening in earnest.

On February 11, 2007, long before the 2008 elections, there ran a piece in The Philadelphia Inquirer, written by Los Angeles Times columnist, Mark Z Barabak, of which the previous quotes were borrowed. Later in the article, Mr. Barabak writes, and I quote him in part, "Obama, 45, the son of a black Kenyan father and a white American mother."

With this stipulation noted, and remembering the questioning of McCain's citizenship, given that he was born in the Panama Canal Zone, wasn't it reasonable to apply the same challenge to Obama. The fact that our media remained unmoved and quiet signals a frightening scenario, given the little "wiggle room" offered when the picture of a Kenyan father is presented as fact. For this to remain under the surface, and to expect that it would for a year and a half, represents a monumental conspiracy coupled with an overall public ignorance.

In view of this colossal deception, is the American voter so apathetic that centuries of legal standings now become secondary in nature? If part of our Constitution is to be ignored so easily, will other sections follow?

The intent of the "natural born citizen" clause was to ensure the highest order of patriotism and loyalty. Parents had to be American citizens at the time of their child's birth. Our Forefathers considered the loyalty factor as being quintessential for being President which in turn, would assure the highest levels of leadership. Our first President, George Washington, personified these qualities.

The future is ours to hold. Good looks and emotions should be left in Hollywood. A record of performance and a professed American loyalty should always top our Presidential considerations. In recent times, the absence of both caused four deaths in Benghazi.

What Matters

April 4, 2015

Where did all this dissension come from? I mean, if one follows the "gay lifestyle," so be it. It's not for me, or hopefully for the majority of Americans, but what matters is in one's nature. We all have to be true to ourselves.

So, this being said, if I as a Christian bake cakes and a gay couple desires me to bake their wedding cake, depending upon my beliefs; my own inner beliefs and in accordance with my Christian upbringing, I have the right as a free American to do what my conscience dictates. Who can argue against this?

And if one does find fault with this, well then, that person is willful in his or her demands. In other words, they have extended the limits of their own freedoms while jeopardizing another's. And it is to this act, this intrusion of thought and will that the injustice occurs.

Recently, Governor Mike Pence of Indiana and Asa Hutchinson of Arkansas were perfectly fine with their state legislature's passing of a newly written Religious Freedom Restoration Act, RFRA, law, to the point that Arkansas's Governor even said, "bring it on." I imagine this was with anticipation of the unrest and protest taking place in Indiana.

Well, overnight, Governor Hutchinson wimped out, supposedly after being influenced by his son. So much for a man's word, his integrity and leadership. This last point, leadership, is all fine and Jim Dandy when things run smoothly. However, its test begins when the stuff hits the fan. As such, both Governors have been found lacking in this regard, which I also suspect is a common weakness with government in general.

Now, from the standpoint of protest, where does all this vitriol come from? From the number of gay friends that I know, it's a "live and let live" style of living. In fact, most are gainfully employed, own their own businesses but with all, their time is too limited for idle "could bes."

It was odd that the first day of protests featured only "hundreds' while the next day, reported numbers were in the "thousands." Could there have been a "get out the vote" effort when sensing the intimidation factor from the excessive amount of media coverage?

It seems to me that in addition to college grads not finding appropriate employment, they are just waiting for the next protest event. After all, their minds have been swept clear of any patriotic or pro-American spirits. Also, they all are well aware of and would like nothing better than to equal those protest legends from the turbulent sixties.

At their young age, they tend to impart a sort of societal conscience, of their own knowing. No longer does government decree laws; it almost seems that controversial legislation must first endure this emotional vetting from the younger set who generally operate by their self-indulgent guidance of "being so sure of what they don't know!"

This type of discourse is not productive nor is it normal as it reflects upon an unsavory societal undercurrent, often driven by the unscrupulous.

In retaliation, we must, in our hearts, recognize our First Amendment rights, which, by their unalienable status are above the reaches of man or man's government. This stipulation of unalienable rights is the separation of American government from those rights of its citizens. And at the core of this unworthy discussion, given its unalienable recognition, is whether free Americans will be willing to uphold and protect their religious beliefs.

As per Christian doctrine, marriage begins with the uniting of one man with one woman. How does one reverse a belief which has been engrained since childhood and has endured throughout the ages, so that marriage can become an affair of anti-Biblical coupling? And is Nature's balance still relevant?

And let us not overlook the totality of Christian bashing, which has evolved in sad fashion during the last couple of decades. There is an ongoing effort to denounce, attack and condemn the cross and all that it represents. Hence, our Holy Christmas season stands out with love and peace against their religious venom.

John Adams, in 1789 warned that "Our Constitution was made for only for a moral and religious people." George Washington believed that "Of all the dispositions and habits which lead to political prosperity, Religion and morality are indispensable supports." And I might add, it's President Washington's capital R not mine.

This debate, from a Christian and Constitutional standpoint, lacks any standing. So as a Christian nation, this is a settled matter. If anything, those that rile up in protest are indeed irreligious and defiant of our nation's most "indispensable supports." As such, are we to bow to such unorthodoxy, such unrestrained demands? If so, when will our Christmas trees become their next object to desecrate?

Democrats Should Be Tense

April 11, 2015

Let me first say that at this early stage, I am a Scott Walker man. Others arouse my interest but as a chief executive of an indebted blue State, his successful election as Governor in addition to his performance is a big deal.

His record of turning the State's budget from red ink to black adds to his resume. Also, the unsuccessful "recall" attempts, for which he gained more numerical support than when originally elected, is a public validation of Walker's success at governing.

Now, after hearing Rand Paul's announcement, coupled with his informal question and answer session in New Hampshire, I now consider the good Senator to be a close second in a growing field which will be jammed full of not only conservatives, but Constitutionalists.

Finally, for once, when thrown the abortion bomb, Sen. Paul glibly threw it right back! His remark which roughly stated, go get the answers first from the DNC and Debbie Wasserman Shultz and then come back and ask me that question again was long overdue! And it's no wonder as to why his commonsense remarks are now being so intricately criticized.

What is eye-opening within this media fury is the identity of the lead attack dog—none other than that fair and balanced dizzy blond moderator Megyn Kelly, who took it upon herself to defend all female journalists from this gender insensitive Republican ruffian. Kelly attempted to reintroduce the dreaded "war on women" play card while also trying to slow down Paul's current momentum.

Kelly was into one of her self-aggrandizing diatribes filled with the appropriate ridicule which such perceived impudence deserved. Given the past Republican ineptness when dealing with the abortion subject, how dare Paul reverse such a gotcha and biased journalistic formula?

Simply put, after hearing his answer yesterday on the internet replay, Paul is worthy and will be taken much more seriously now. No longer will Candy Crowley's style of attack and ridicule, when interviewing or moderating, be tolerated. This was truly an American moment since the liberal press was finally put on notice.

I suppose this reaction lingers from when Ms. Crowley intervened to save Obama's skin during her infamous 2012 moderating bit. It still stings and today it's been coupled with Sen. Reid's recent boasting that he lied in order to help re-elect Obama. However, both instances are now overshadowed by the Democrat's lead candidate. Her record of zero accomplishments falls flat against the probable candidacy of Gov. Walker. When considering Sen. Paul's rising credibility, it becomes increasingly clear that this democrat reign will finally run its course. Necessity, common sense and truth will play to "standing room only" crowds.

Still, it's almost a certainty that Hillary's broomstick will be thrown into the next Presidential round. Despite her total lack of accomplishments, at any level of government, she is within days of throwing her two cents into the 2016 campaign.

This insult will supposedly be presented over the weekend. In a fair size intro type of article by AP's Julie Pace and Ken Thomas, the thought is that Hillary will officially declare on a small and personal scale this Sunday morning.

Quotes within the Pace/Thomas report attempt to clean up this leftover from the sixties. Sylvia Larsen, a New Hampshire State Democrat offered that, "When people meet Hillary Clinton, they are persuaded." And Davenport Iowa Mayor Bill Gluba, another Hillary supporter, attempted the impossible with, "She's a very decent wonderful woman."

The point to all this is what happened to credibility, to a proven record with a list of accomplishments? Is it really just about name recognition, coupled with the fluff treatment from an adoring media?

Not only is her entrance a disgrace, given her flare for scandals and future testifying dates, this media treatment is insufferable.

At this point, the mere fact that Hillary will become the Democrat's lead contender says volumes. Other credible Republican have yet to officially join the race but for me, Walker, who has yet to announce, and Paul are candidates worthy of the burden of leadership which the Presidency requires.

A Rare Comparison

April 26, 2015

Just for kicks, sad kicks but kicks none-the-less, could it be as simple as comparing quotes from our former 2012 Presidential contest? As Confucius famously said, "A man simply cannot conceal himself" And with the following comments, that bit if aged wisdom sheds it all!

As many were made aware of by all the dotting coverage, last night was Washington's go around trying to emulate Hollywood. Such was its black-tie affair known as The Correspondent's Dinner. However, down the coast from the Potomac power elite, an earlier event took place in Florida with the Jacksonville University's graduation ceremonies.

Obviously, our esteemed and self-proclaimed prestigious President captured the evening's coverage in the prior event while his humble 2012 Presidential contender imparted some useful advice to the class of recent graduates during the second affair.

Given the different approach to both events, it is understandable as to the diverse nature of speech and spontaneity. One was a festive mixture of amply dispersing ridicule with self-aggrandizing while the other was more of a solemn occasion honoring the rights of passage from student onto assuming the responsible share of citizenship.

At the dinner, Obama quipped that he is "determined to make the most of every moment I have left." Depending upon one's perspective, this comment either startled or saddened many in attendance. However, his downturn occurred as his comic side took over. When revealing that his advisors had asked if he had a bucket list, Our President's reply was, "Well, I have something that rhymes with bucket list." Could it be that a chuckle or two was heard emanating from Jane Fonda, as she too remembered a list from long ago?

This brand of humor should be reserved to a comic's nightclub skits, it should not be uttered by one who commands our military and is the leader of our United States and the free world!

Mitt Romney on the other hand, and given the solemnity of his occasion, remained as his usual Presidential self. Addressing the newly minted graduates and their families, Mitt advised, "Get a life, have a life, live your life in full. Embrace every fruitful dimension of life that you possibly can." Also, he added, "If your life is lived for money and position, it will be shallow and unfulfilling." He concluded with, "And for the sake of preserving Freedom, vote. Please vote."

Understanding that the different atmosphere of each event offered greater latitudes of expression in the former rather than the latter, still, as our President, one might expect a higher degree of conduct by a more innocent level of humor and classy oratory.

Obama is sadly still the President of our Country at home and abroad. In leadership positions, there is this universal expectation for a particular persona, an etiquette denoting acceptable conduct which is inherent to his highly elected station.

Since our unfortunate re-election, many have mused over what would have been if? I think that yesterday's display revealed the chasm which keeps this wondering alive. Given the opportunity, Obama gravitated into his most natural and comfortable thinking. Romney on the other hand cared for and tried to offer useful insights from his own experiences in life. As stated, this was predicated upon the diverse settings so such a comparison may be unjust.

It should be no secret that this writing has been from a Romney voter yet I'm just wondering if the laughter that Obama no doubt received was so rewarding that if the events were reversed, would his format have changed.

Actually, such two differing portrayals offer a realistic telltale, a residue from what the choices were in 2012. A polished, reserved, humble and greatly successful businessman verses a street corner hustler who mesmerized the press corps into his lock step adoration.

A True Public Servant Will Prevail

September 27, 2015

Governor Walker's early exit speech contained this telling piece of advice; "I encourage other Republican Presidential candidates to consider doing the same so the voters can focus on a limited number of candidates who can offer a positive conservative alternative to the current front-runner." He apparently thinks that only a professional politician can offer a "positive conservative alternative." How infuriating when it is the career public servant who brought and built this ineptness into our government?

Also, three candidates own asterisks after their names based upon the Constitution's term of "natural born citizen" (NBC), with the only exception being "a citizen of the United States, at the time of this Constitution…" This lofty requirement for those seeking our Presidency holds a stiffer degree of eligibility, as it should.

The difference between "a citizen" versus the distinction of NBC was erased for those "citizens who were "grandfathered" by soldiering against the British, therefore proving their allegiance through their service and sacrifice. Still, the distinction of NBC originally and to this day required both parents to be citizens at the time of the candidate's birth. This was to ensure the highest possible degree of American allegiance.

This allegiance issue was "prime time" back during the 1960 elections, when JFK was doubted, despite his WWII heroics. Voters questioned his candidacy simply based upon his Roman Catholic faith, which was believed to include an allegiance to the Pope. This dual allegiance question was a hotbed issue fifty-five years ago but today, few are even aware of this legal regard which maintains the upmost allegiance in our Presidential candidates.

For our Forefathers, it was all about allegiance and placing the qualifying bar at its highest pinnacle so as to ensure the upmost faithful and loyal service, in addition to one's proven leadership and personal fidelity.

This election offers much to consider. Not only are these newcomers, these outsiders, appealing, but we also have to determine what is worth preserving since there is an effort to minimize our Founding and to erase our Judeo-Christian heritage. This theory became public with Obama's statement that America is not a Christian nation.

So, this maintaining of the stiffest of election standards should provide a pro American administration. In agreement, Dr. Carson recently stated, "I would not advocate that we put a Muslim in charge of this nation." I might add that despite media attempts to generate a public outcry against the good doctor's position, we all remember the 9/11 pictures of those jumping to their deaths! However, Dr. Carson's concern centers solely upon the preservation of American allegiance.

Dare we remember when a former draft dodger not only campaigned, but gained his party's nomination and was then elected and re-elected as our "Commander-in-Chief. When also assessing today's version of this Commander-in Chief, it is clear that the American brand which Trump offers is long overdue and critically needed.

Initially, I supported and donated to Gov. Walker's campaign. However, after listening to Walker's farewell, I am glad that he dropped out since his thoughts only seem to focus upon his political brethren. It's almost as if he is murmuring, "how dare those outsiders." Well, the outsider's brash and honest talk has captured the hearts of many voters.

What may well be the defining issue of this campaign season could actually be Trump's hot button anchor baby issue since only Trump bought up how, over the years, our 14th Amendment has been reinterpreted into a completely different design its original purpose. This daring of an issue so long ignored, came from an outsider, a businessman and not from a career politician!

This challenge to what has become an accepted standard is what caught my attention. Imagine for a moment how Cruz, with his high legal profile and Constitutional prowess, could still choose to bypass this Constitutional abuse. This sort of go-along acceptance is in part what our government has for too long produced while ignoring any attempt at Constitutional allegiance.

To emphasize, it is the career politician who does not want to rock the boat. It is the career politician who has engineered our Country's failings. It is the career politician who exhorts during the campaign season only to forget during one's term of office. It is the career politician which now takes umbrage when a few concerned and capable citizens compete in their field of "expertise." And finally, it is the career politician who intentionally is out of step with the tune that most citizens are singing.

The catalyst which has generated Trump's huge following is the reaction to the indifference which both Houses of Congress have displayed. At this point, there will be a new direction taken in 2016 since those entrusted with our faith have not only failed but have brazenly ignored their obligations.

Just as with the media's ongoing undressing, so will the political establishment experience the public's long overdue wake up. An outsider will win the Presidency and in doing so will usher in a new and productive standard. Its precedence, when successful, should endure longer than expected.

America's Crumbling Character

October 25, 2015

Given the fact that four Americans died needlessly in the service of our Country, other sinister players became evident during Clinton's arrogant Benghazi testimony.

First, if anyone is still unclear as to which party plays the Congressional obstructionist role, such wonderings have been answered. Just how in hell can an investigation be conducted when all five democrat members of the Benghazi panel care more about Hillary's political viability and Presidential ambitions than in discovering the facts which led to our American losses?

This despicable display of democrat partisanship, especially given the stakes involved, should have been a lesson for all Americans. Even without Harry Reid's obstructionist leadership, Cummings's panel presented the viewing public with what actually is the more responsible player of congressional gridlock. That being the agenda of the democrat party over the purposeful needs of our country.

Those five democrats lick booted their way with their salutary "madam secretary" openings rather than offering a respectful line of questions concerning the events of that night. Instead, these panel members fell over themselves with either words praising their "madam secretary" or uttering apologies for a previous inquiry from their political counterparts.

Even so, Clinton still became cornered in a timeline issue. A Wall Street Journal editorial reported that Representative Trey Gowdy "released hitherto undisclosed documents showing that Mrs. Clinton believed from the start that the attack was perpetrated by terrorists. At 11:12 p.m. on the night of the attack, Clinton emailed her daughter Chelsea that 'Two of our officers were killed in Benghazi by Al Queda-like group" This definitive statement reveals her understanding of the true cause while at the same time, she continued to tell the American public her video fable. Obviously, she was caught and proven to be an open- and bold-faced public liar!

In a supportive role, and while completely dismissing Clinton's email gaffe to her daughter, media accounts characterized the session as "congressional grilling" and that Clinton "held her ground in calm fashion." On Saturday, the Wall Street Journal ran an article entitled, Clinton Momentum Builds After Challenging Week. This type of disrespectful prose has sadly become the norm from what increasingly appears to be a supportive government agency, ready to aid any and all progressives, no matter what.

Are we to believe that Clinton's responsibilities are now behind her after only one day of questioning? And how about all the accounts reporting that her questioning lasted eleven hours? Really? I seem to remember at least a one-hour lunch break and then there was that longer interruption so that panel members could comply with their official voting duties. So, while technically the hearing spanned eleven hours, to report that Clinton's "grilling" totaled that time is intentionally false and misleading; in reality, somewhere between eight and nine hours, maybe.

While the time objection may seem a bit trifling, it's woven into this continuing Clinton mystic, which has been fine-tuned over time. However, just where is the media's conscience, or for that matter, much of the publics? Are four lives so easily discarded in preference to one's whimsical desires for a "first" woman President? Was her husband's tour gratifying or worthy?

Back in the day, President Clinton's major stumbling block of dodging our Nation's draft, in a time of war, was quickly swept away with his looks and his "good ole boy" country appeal as few realized the price of such fantasies. Are we now ready to forgive or worse, forget, what took place on that 9/11 night in Benghazi? After three damn long years, are certain interests waiting for the statute of limitations to kick in? If so, be informed that for murder, this is not applicable.

Look around and do your own self appraisal. How many friends and family members have secure employment, or are even gainfully employed? And how far does the weekly paycheck stretch today? Then, of course, that promise of "free" health care has only resulted in higher premiums!

We have been promised the moon for too long. Life isn't about freebies nor is it about ignoring accountability. At least, not in the long run, since life's own accounting process has a way of evening the score.

Read all the glowing accounts of Mrs. Clinton's "calm fashion" if you must but we have already experienced the results from false promising and rosy predictions. What is waiting in the wings is more of the same! Despite all the spin and re-interpreting that one digests, the fact remains that Clinton lied to our people and to the families of those that were slain. Addressing the nation is one thing but to stand eyeball to eyeball with grieving family members, while promising them what you know to be untrue, well, that's a special kind of cold.

Finally, consider her two separate communications; the first to her daughter while the attack still raged and then with the Egyptian Prime Minister the next afternoon, in which she states, "We know that the attack in Libya had nothing to do with the film. It was a planned attack – not a protest."

The official position of the Obama Administration continued to identify the video as being the culprit. So, does the Egyptian Prime Minister's faith in America falter when listening to Obama's video claim while still remembering Clinton's conflicting message? This is just one result which validates why our American Presidency must be held to its highest standards. Liars need not apply!

Honoring Thanksgiving Day First

November 20, 2015

Think about it people; those who fracture our seasonal Christmas joy with their secular "happy holiday" nonsense now seem composed of a new mindset that employs this premature and overlapping Christmas emphasis, to the exclusion of our traditional day of Thanksgiving. Has our American culture become that easily manipulated?

In days past, Christmas displays didn't even appear till December, as Thanksgiving was given its just respect from American families and for all the Blessings which God has presented throughout the year. Later, the significance of Christmas was celebrated through its religious context rather than today's more commercial version.

Today, America is witnessing the beginnings of an effort to devalue our family gatherings around the turkey. This Blessed holiday, denoting thankful prayer, unity and humble tidings is now being marginalized through this disrespectful extension of what Christians consider to be their most religious time of the year, the precious birth of Christ.

At this point, after years of witnessing the trendy neutering of Christmas, with displaying clear lights rather than the traditional bulbs of green and red, and with listening to shoppers wishing each other's "happy holidays" rather than "Merry Christmas," I now wonder about our Muslim counterparts and how alterations to their basic religious traditions and beliefs would be taken by their believers.

Clearly, there is a transition taking place across America when Nativity scenes inspire public protests. In fact, throughout the year, displays of our Ten Commandments yield identical reactions.

I hear it all the time; "Times are changing," or "that's old school." This shift is not only amazing time wise, but alarming considering its ease of acceptance. At this point, we must hold sacred to our beliefs while instilling these principles onto our young. If not, there will come a time when we truly will not be a Christian Nation.

Our Thanksgiving Day observances came about during the days of President Washington. If I may recount from Washington's October 3, 1789, Thanksgiving Proclamation in part:

> "Whereas it is the duty of all Nations to acknowledge the providence of Almighty God, to obey his will, to be grateful for his benefits, and humbly to implore his protection and favor, and Whereas both Houses of Congress have by their joint Committee requested me "to recommend to the People of the United States a day of public thanks-giving and prayer to be observed by acknowledging with grateful hearts the many signal favors of Almighty God, especially by affording them an opportunity peaceably to establish a form of government for their safety and happiness."

In this, Washington's opening paragraph, he mentions points that have already become trite among modern thinkers, essayists and also with a large portion of Americans. Yet his words reflect the assumed normalcy of America's citizenry; a devotion to God and Country, an obedience to morality and conscience coupled with a self-righteousness regarding his fellow man. While viewed as insignificant or out of step with today's America, this approach may have spurred our present-day lack of respect and appreciation for what preceded.

Washington cites "the duty of all Nations." Today, we dismiss obeying "his will," or "to be grateful for his benefits," since many in our computerized society find it uncomfortable to even acknowledge God's being. Also, Washington mentioned in his 1796 Farewell Address, "Of all the dispositions and habits which lead to political prosperity, Religion and morality are indispensable supports."

These words from both oratories may hold clues to what ails our current haplessness. Especially when we have re-elected a President who dismisses the notion that America is a Christian Nation? Are we still capable of readopting this useful insight from our Founders?

Our first President also mentions how fortunate we were to be able to "establish a form of government for their safety and happiness." Simply stated, and even more so expected, was Washington's assumption that our people's safety would be had by government's most sacred trust and duty.

Once again, there seems to be a hitch to our get along. The same President who doubts our Christian bearing also refuses to answer our Constitution's call for protection "against invasion." Each State joined our Union with a guarantee of becoming part of a larger and more protective entity. However, in today's version of liberty and justice, more interest and care are afforded to the foreign invader or refugee than to our natural born.

All this should make one realize that our Nation cannot continue with her bleeding. We are Americans and what we have inherited is far more worthy than the future which will await us all. As our Forefathers pointed out, it's "we the people." And it's "we the people," of which the vast majority are still Christians, who continue in silence when being wished "happy holidays." Again, maybe trivial and insignificant but then with that mindset, what isn't?

One Amazing Man

December 2, 2015

With ever increasing rage arising from our intellectual centers over income inequality, can we pause long enough to ask one question? That being, "why would a billionaire want to become our President?" I mean, forgetting all his wealth and successful business acumen, what would motivate Trump to get down into the political garbage of a presidential campaign?

Why hasn't one single editorial or talk show star taken up this very relevant question? Could it be that Donald Trump really and truly loves America? Aside from all his wealth and luxurious living, could there be more to this man than brash replies, private jets and charity golfing events? In all probability, this has been answered since what else could justify such an extended effort and willingness for sacrifice?

As it stands now, Mr. Trump has become a thorn to many, but this discomfort is being felt solely by those who have earned the displeasure. It is to these individuals, those with RINO attached to their names that seem bedeviled by Trump's lasting appeal.

If it weren't such a critical time for America, this drama would be somewhat amusing. Here is a candidate that defies all. In modern America, our "free press" employs whatever means necessary for determining the success or failure of a candidate. For those who doubt, refer to Herman Cain; however, not so with Mr. Trump.

The media has come to a standstill since every condemnation only adds to his support. As previously mentioned, this brick wall has become an enjoyable surprise, especially since our media flaunts its political bias with a bullish influence.

Another humorous venue worthy of our attention is the "establishment's" roster of poster boys. With all the fanfare and expectations of a much-needed savior, Jeb Bush opened their bid but never hit double digits. In clumsy fashion, he neutralized all his financial backing and endorsements when supporting both open immigration and the common core curriculum. As such, the establishment has begun to fade. And with the same flighty manner as a flirtatious schoolgirl, these shadow players reshuffled and are now beginning to wager on another Floridian, Marco Rubio.

This was a natural alternative, given what a dream candidate Rubio is! Here, wrapped in one package is a handsome Latino, owning a rags-to-riches portfolio comparable to Dr. Carson's tale. With a gift to gab, reminiscent of another slick talking single term Senator, Rubio impresses his newly found backers. However, what is conveniently overlooked is his parentage. Our Constitution explicitly states that only a "natural born citizen" can become President of the United States. As was the case in 2008, this once again is being ignored by our press.

Already, the purpose of maintaining the highest degree of allegiance should have been validated by the last seven years of an anti-American Presidency. Certainly, with this experience so freshly engrained, what our Forefathers viewed as so important should now hold the greatest of value.

For the curious, these pre-primary months offer a behind the scenes look-see of the scheming and preferences by the unseen players; those with the bucks and the inside track to the top echelons of our government. Most obvious has been this recent shift from Bush to Rubio. Left unmentioned are the benchwarmers, if needed, of Kasich and Christie.

The outcasts Trump, Carson, and Carly are from the private sector. The only politico to be lumped with this trio is the outspoken Cruz, who sadly happens to own the same parental disqualifications, as Rubio.

And try as they might, our dysfunctional media continues with its futile attempts to scandalize Trump. Recently, their ploy centered upon Trump's statement that thousands of Muslims were celebrating our 9/11 losses. While they ranted and raved over this, their silence is deafening since learning of statements collaborating Trump's 9/11 beliefs. Bernie Kerik, NYC chief of police, along with Rudy Giuliani have voiced support of Trump's claim.

Another element to Trump's popularity is that he hits the public's pulse. Once again, he has raised an issue which will be a home run. Trump has stated that he believes that our children should be able to pray in school. This is a winning issue which will no doubt infuriate the establishment.

Trump remains on top because Trump is a proud American who believes in his Country. He taps into what, in many cases, has been judicially muscled away from our inalienable beings. What is needed is for every red blooded American to do his or her best in his behalf.

In many aspects, he is a God send; much in the same manner which our Forefathers often praised His Devine Intervention during critical moments of our war for independence. They took advantage of His gifts, and we must do the same!

Trump's Surprising Foe

January 4, 2016

Four days into the New Year and already Trump has deflated all hopes and expectations of his quick departure. Some rated his candidacy as an ego booster while others cavalierly pointed to it just being an expensive hobby. At this point, I think the above is nothing more than foolishness since he may well be the Republican nominee!

So, at this juncture, the question becomes; what is Trump's stiffest competition? Most would name Hillary and that would be wrong! The answer to this great question contains only four letters, RINO. His greatest pushback will come from his own people, essentially, the Republican establishment.

With Obama's original 2008 success and subsequent re-election, the political imaging within the Republican ranks has undergone a sort of fracturing, a realignment. Almost immediately, their 2008 champion left many deflated and glum. McCain was neither popular nor able for the demands of campaigning. His selection of Sarah Palin only underlined his Dole-like candidacy.

Follow that up with the out of nowhere emergence of the Tea Party. To the establishment, its sudden emerging influence gave way to dire hopes that these upstarts would die of a quick and timely death. Not so.

Then, the Republican's unknown and shadowy shenanigans became unveiled when out of the shadows emerged their RINO identities. After decades of wondering why nothing ever seemed to change, no matter who was elected, this one awakening of the back room deals and the unnamed and mysterious players seemed to give voters the missing link.

As a result of this new public awareness, Republican leadership has become more responsive, or at east more aware of its conduct, appearances and loyalty. There is a higher level of public expectation for accountability when realizing that along with the usual Democrat reluctance, another factor is clogging the gears.

Think back for a moment to the pre-Obama-George Bush days. It was a period prior to RINO awareness or Tea Party unity; a time that for all our hopes and desires, nothing seemed to change. While Obama won in 2008, his "elections have consequences" quip now applies more than ever.

The final injury to the Republican art of compromise came in the persona of Donald Trump. Again, out of nowhere, when events were running as expected, one of their own, a highly successful businessman who normally and should only be concerned with acquiring more money emerged.

Here was an American, who by all accounts was not even a bonafide conservative, having only joined the Republican ranks after voting for Obama in 2008. Why and how dare this billionaire enter into what is none of his business? And he's supposedly from their ranks! So, as one month drags into many, those moneyed people, along with the Republican leadership are now in a quandary since they consider Trump to be an uninvited guest. More to the point and despite all their behind-the-scenes ploys, for the first time, they are sensing their helpless state. So, Trump's most formidable opponent comes from his own ranks, both found within the political and corporate sectors.

As 2016 unfolds with the usual slate of primaries and subsequent news reports, it is becoming obvious that candidate Trump regards his political adversary, namely Clinton, to be more of an itch than a threat. Enlisting her husband's ole boy campaign charm both validates her floundering campaign while providing Trump with more than enough ammunition.

While Obama has been a total Constitutional disaster, he has brought beneficial revelations to our frustrated conservative base. Since 2008, he is the reason for all this innovation and change. Without his anti-American defiance I doubt if our energy would be what it is today.

America stands at her abyss. We need a saving reversal and quickly. Trump offers that opportunity like no other since he is above corruptive influences. The best judgment of his potential Presidency comes from those that are aligned against him; especially as so many are from the previously unknown RINO ranks!

In The Nick of Time

October 3, 2016

With roughly a month remaining before the elections, the democrat candidate has yet to inform her supporters about her policy positions. Still the media finds this and her 250-day-plus absence from press conferences to be no big deal. This lack of involvement is a sad replay of her past disinterest concerning calls for additional security in Benghazi. And that too was glossed over by our media stars.

The media's disinterested approach suggests that the democrat party has endorsed someone who is without the basic essentials for leadership. In this context, little wonder as to why our media is fixated solely upon Clinton's past so-called "experience" rather than to exhort her accomplishments.

This insight differs sharply from the flowery writing of Wall Street Journal columnist Dorothy Rabinowitz. While she no doubt resides in Clinton's corner, her praise is somewhat confusing when citing Clinton assets as: "experienced, forward looking, indomitably determined and eminently sane." This in contrast to her ridicule of Trump as "the most unstable, proudly uninformed, psychologically unfit president ever."

However, in the grand scheme of things, the scheme is all that matters. Clinton merely fills a need. The heart of the matter is to ensure that the status quo is maintained. So obviously, Trump must be maligned and destroyed in whatever fashion available.

One such method shores up Clinton's vulnerabilities as public attention becomes sidetracked. Nothing is ever won on defense, so the attack mantra is now focusing upon Trump's shortcomings, and with particular emphasis upon his 'alfa dog' nature. As such, the playbook of personal attack has become her favorite weapon.

This unorthodox journalism is defensive so that all which the establishment has accomplished during the last one hundred years will be preserved. This intent is reflective of what truly matters in governmental circles; it's the establishment and its bureaucratic agenda which comes before Country. This is central to our current refugee situation. While it is difficult to justify this open-door policy, if national security was still in play, it now abides by the establishment's designs.

A differing perspective casts the Trump candidacy through the prism of betrayal. Obvious is the fact that as a billionaire "player," with a history of government dealing at all levels, he walked among the elites and the captains of industry, both here and abroad. As such, he was and remains well aware of the game and its insider rules. This is tantamount to his perceived turn coat status.

And now, his candidacy includes the dismantling of that structural power grid. He knows the game and has vowed to eliminate elitism's crippling effects. So, is there any wonder or any limit as to what may be hurled against him? Simply stated, the stakes in this scheme are nationally and globally intertwined. Also, there can never be another Brexit!

The possible success of Trump would bring a restructuring of America's balance, both around the world and here at home. In response, many have stepped out of the shadows and revealed their loyalties. Both sides of the aisle are complicit since GOP functionaries have been tagged as RINOs and by their own designs and shenanigans, have earned this distinction.

From the public side of the ledger, we see rising taxes without results; infrastructure that was supposedly "shovel ready" and now an open border policy which includes our acceptance of Islamic terrorists. In response, is our frustrated refrain that "our immigration laws are broken." What law wouldn't be broken if it weren't enforced?

This Presidential election features one candidate wanting to end America's downward slide while the other will grease the skids. For too long, certain issues have intentionally remained unnoticed and ignored. Policies such as "anchor babies," which contribute to the establishment's scheme, will now be addressed through a proper Constitutional rendering. Needless to say, before Trump, these issues were treated as political "third rails."

Think about the many past promises for a secure border and how open it remains! Also, who would have endorsed this insane policy of granting instant citizenship based upon illegal entry and subsequent birth? Our Constitution is not in the business of rewarding criminal actions.

Finally, consider the growing $2 billion debt per day, failing schools, unwinnable wars against lesser enemies, continuation of corporate flight and of legislating and judicially confirming the legality of compelling free Americans to buy a product that he or she neither wants, needs nor can afford. Then, "taxing" those same "free" Americans for not purchasing? And they still wonder what caused Trump's following and his groundswell of support? Given our current anti-American slide, Trump's emergence seems to be in the nick of time!

A No-Brainer Choice

October 15, 2016

What is there to decide? One the one hand, a proven winner in business, who cannot be bought or intimidated, versus an inept individual who has failed at everything she attempts. At this point, this last debate seems, at best, anti-climactic.

Dare we compare the enthusiastic "packed houses" of stadium sized venues verses Hillary's school gymnasium gatherings? More important is the contrast of a love for Country which embellishes throughout versus the giveaway programs flavored with shrieks of gender inequality and racial discord.

Glaring is her message's limited appeal since efforts are mainly focused upon college campuses. What better arena to spew the impossible than to those who listen daily to whimsical classroom lecturing? For the huckster, the one who can't carnival bark the same incentives to those who know better, this setting is a natural.

What hangs in the balance is not so much who wins but what the results will be. If the status quo is preferable, then Clinton gets the nod. However, when recalling what America was before the nineties versus today, the Trump choice becomes a no-brainer.

He also presents a unique persona since who of his financial level could nor would venture into the slime of politics? He might be the only billionaire to retain his love of country over a love for money, wealth and luxury. Think about it, his patriotism and his sincere caring for working Americans is the exception, a rarity from those wealthy ranks.

Consequently, recent developments have aroused public curiosity and general disbelief. Who knew about the abuse of Congressional checking accounts or even the accounts themselves? And how about the RINO's unmasking and the public's present disregard concerning the media's pro-Hillary blathering. It's now evident that our media is a Clinton cohort and is wielded by the establishment as a propaganda tool, which also benefits our federal government.

The "establishment" views a Trump victory with the same fear Dracula would if caught in the sunshine or when facing a cross. This is the first time ever that America's unseen network has been threatened. As such, and with all that is riding on the outcome, in addition to electing a President, November 8th will determine the fate of our Country. Between now and then, the unknowns, those whose power broke within that cherished "establishment" will do whatever it takes, even with dusting off those slanderous charges heaved against Herman Cain four years prior. These shadow dwellers care only in preserving the agenda to which they have serviced, worshipped and obeyed since the early days of the last century.

We are fortunate that the plotters of America's decline, led by many at the Council on Foreign Relations (CFR), got impatient. This might have been hurried from the fear of imitating that Brexit vote. Also demanding were the numbers which these weasels assumed spelled a numerical superiority. However, within each Trump rally, a movement or if you like, an American awakening, is taking place which now includes hundreds of thousands of democrats supporting Trump.

Our enemies have long anticipated our decline and for obvious reasons. We have revised our own standards into a sort of wishy-washy grab bag of emotional peeves and watered down traditions. Those watching do not ignore the folly from our electing inept and anti-American leadership.

Consider our past futility against unworthy communist foes, the removal of prayer/Bible from our classrooms, or when electing a commander-in-chief who was a documented draft-dodger. Also, Washington's refusal to enforce our borders, America's racial harmony becoming pierced and now we have a national debt that threatens our solvency. The quality of our past and current leadership, in addition to a Clinton continuation of such, has juiced up the CFR's timetable.

Clinton's election is considered, by the establishment's hierarchy, as a mere formality leading to a total takeover of America's governing power. Our state is such that the shadows believe that in the election's aftermath, America is for the taking.

Fortunately, Americans seem to be grasping the realization that yes, there are shadows, and that darkness is anti-American. In one respect, certain elements have self-revealed due to their own impatience. Most glaring is the unrepentant prose of the pro-Hillary media. At this point, they even consider their "liberal" pretense to be excess baggage. This may explain the additional reference to the supersecret George Soros. He has waited a lifetime for America's final vulnerability.

In approximately three weeks we have a decision to make about America's future. Will it be a candidate who recently stated, "deep seated cultural codes, religious beliefs and structural biases have to be changed" or will our American heritage and present-day condition be better served by a President who vows to "make America Great again?" Talk about a no brainer!

No More of This

November 1, 2016

Realizing that there is a significant number of voters who were too young for Hillary Clinton's earlier escapades, maybe a review would protect the unsuspecting from being hoodwinked by Clinton's current verbiage.

Slightly over twenty years ago, on June 11, 1996, columnist Steve Dunleavy wrote a piece in the New York Post which opened with an appropriate word to both Clintons: "Unbelievable."

For those too young, to recall when Clinton was first becoming President in January 1993, the White House Travel Office came under the intense scrutiny from First Lady, Hillary Clinton. An effort commenced to replace its chief, Billy Dale and his staff; a person who for over 32 years, loyally and efficiently served both Republican and Democrat Administrations.

This undertaking ultimately included, as Mr. Dunleavy describes, "one of the most venal acts that the Clinton White House ever perpetrated." These abusive actions of slander and even criminal charges were set in motion simply "because Hillary wanted to put her cronies in the Travel Office."

Previously, an article from the Los Angeles Times entitled, White House received FBI files on ex-travel aide, was featured on June 6, 1996, in The Philadelphia Inquirer which identified one particular Hillary crony, Hollywood producer Mr. Harry Thomason, who as the report states, "had been lobbying the President for a share of the travel business."

In their effort to replace Dale, another incident erupted. This was to become known as "Filegate." Somehow, as Dunleavy writes, "the White House improperly got personal FBI files on 341 prominent Republicans. In response, a "bureaucratic bungle" was the given excuse. Supposedly, this occurred, as Dunleavy details, "when Clinton realized that Hillary might have gone too far in 'the hit' on Dale, so they went to the feds to construct a climate of infamy around the poor guy."

As The Times reported, "Dale and six other office staff members were fired on May 19th, 1993, allegedly for mismanagement of the office...." Later, "President Clinton acknowledged the dismissals were a mistake and offered the workers new jobs."

This brief glimpse has examined just one of the many sandals which earmarked the Clinton presidency, and will no doubt resurface if another Clinton re-enters the Oval Office. Yet there is so much more that remains pertinent to current events.

An LA Times piece began with, "The White House improperly used the FBI for political purposes by obtaining confidential files on the White House travel director seven months after he was fired." Now this is a vendetta type of "nasty!" And the plot thickens of the files by the White House was improper."

Insight from Hillary's target, Mr. Dale details even more. Commenting on the 341 victims of Clinton, as was reported, "FBI Director Louis B. Freeh disputed the notion that the use's illegal search and seizure efforts, Dale stated that "these are people who were mostly advanced people. People who might be volunteers, some of them getting paid per diem or some who were paid for a few weeks work."

When asked about their relevance, Dale offered, "Well, these are the people who you can single out, track them down and say to them: 'Hey, you did some work for so-and-so. What was he like?' In other words, people who are very ripe for leaks about a person's personal or private life."

The slanderous approach and criminal charges leveled at Mr. Dale so long ago have resurfaced in our mainstream headlines concerning Trump. These people are not leaders; they are unethical and immoral bullies with power. For those who missed those Clinton years, this was just a sampling of what many of us endured and would again become common place with another Clinton Presidency.

It is a fact that Clinton is responsible for what is taking place so close to Election Day. And for those who may have had a change of heart after Comey's recent announcement, just maybe former FBI Director Freeh's past denial of "improper" file use could be pertinent to this current Director's support for a Clinton!

Long ago, statesman Lord Acton remarked that, "power corrupts, and absolute power corrupts absolutely." Now when the unworthy or corrupt gain office, the results are guaranteed. Ironically, Lord Acton pinned the tail on the Clinton donkey quite accurately!

Discounting the emotions of days past, the unbelievable fact of electing a commander-in-chief, who "dodged" our Nation's draft, immediately lowered the standard of the American Presidency. Now his wife, who by her own actions has brought about this election crisis, will no doubt double down with her flare for the lawless.

Her performance will always obliterate her promises. When reviewing their past actions, the expectation for accountability comes in second to their stand-by of "I can't recall," "what difference does it make," "I didn't inhale" or "I'm going to say this just once. I didn't have" All voters must realize that American leadership demands more! Our time is on the eighth to do so!

A Hundred-Year-Old Lesson

November 20, 2016

In the aftermath of our latest Presidential Election, both the disheartened democrats and their jubilant counterparts have been imparting a better election format idea; namely, our Electoral College system is now considered to be antiquated.

So, with this modern-day criticism being leveled against such a proven presidential election prescription, maybe we need to step back and realize how well this formula from our Founders has worked and why it remains applicable. Also, before exercising such a hasty and trendy revision, might we review another promoted constitutional change which supposedly would be an improvement over what was deemed passé?

Prior to the 1913 watershed year of change, each State selected its Senators by their respective State legislators. It was a time when Senators were considered their State's ambassadors to the Federal authority. Our Founders called this system "indirect representation." In other words, the people elected their state legislators, who in turn selected two Senators to represent their State. Therefore, this system connected the people "indirectly" which explains the previous terminology and defines its overall accountability.

These Senators were directly answerable to their state government so when budget time rolled around, care was given not to exceed the federal revenue, which was solely gained from tariffs and excise taxes. If that total happened to exceed the available funds, each State would be accessed, according to its population. Compare that to the opposite and irresponsible direction in which funding flows today!

Under this system, it is obvious that the Senators wo0uld take care not to return home with the unwanted news of needing additional funds since this would raise the question of being replaced. Thus, responsible spending at the federal level was assured through the Senator's accounting to their state legislators.

Today, should we ask; what caused this $20 trillion debt? The answer contains three words, the Seventeenth Amendment! With its ratification in 1913, accountability of the State's ambassadors, i.e. Senators was eliminated by the Amendment's opening sentence; "The Senate of the United States shall be composed of two senators from each state, elected by the people thereof."

Gone was the State legislator's dismal view of federal budget overrides. With the Seventeenth's passing, it came down to a popular vote for the favorite. Senators now only had to appeal to their constituents rather than to their knowledgeable and thrifty State overseers, who in turn were responsible to their districts back home.

The promotion of such a dramatic change centered upon a public appeal for a more direct participation when selecting Senators. The chant was along the lines of, we should have more say in our representation. No thought was directed to the other House of Congress which is appropriately labeled "the people's House." It is here where the people's voice is heard as they directly vote into office their representatives.

This scheme came about based upon two factors. First, it is clear that the Senators would much rather serve under a less accountable system. Secondly, even though this was one hundred years ago, either the people were easily swayed, or they were unknowing of the reasoning and purpose for their government's structure. In either case, they voted for less accountable representation, which is directly responsible for today's current indebtedness.

As noted earlier, in today's post-election time, there is an attempt to generate support for doing away with America's Electoral College. Included, but not as glaring, this would also require the elimination of our individual State elections. However, what is missing is the familiarization of our Electoral College and the reasoning for it. There is more at stake than the eradication of the College itself. If only equal consideration would have preceded the public's support of that 1913 sham!

These post-election times provide the perfect emotional climate for such ignorant proposals. Another example of such counterproductive or in this case, dangerous drives is this decades long push for a "Convention of the States," or simply, a "Con-Con."

Experience should be the teacher that guards against all such promotions that the government suggests. This is expected for when government grows, it begins to exist for its own benefit, being its own master, rather than its stated purpose of preserving our God given rights and freedoms.

So, given this truism, plus remembering the sales pitch preceding the Seventeenth's passage, caution should prevail. Likewise, when voices implore the need for a national or "popular vote" Presidential outcome, it would behoove us to first research. One hundred years ago, no one took time to first learn of the reasoning behind the Founder's "indirect representation" safeguard. That lack of curiosity back then has now cost America over $20 trillion!

The Limits of Fake News

December 2, 2016

Now it's the internet's "fake news" which turned the voters! Really? How hypocritical can this disingenuous profession become? If it wasn't for their ageless reliance for re-inventing the facts, the so-called mainstream media (MSM), or ore to the point, this "fake news" behemoth would fold.

How many of us relished the media's red faces from the Brexit vote? Odd reaction from the supposed guard dogs of truth. Turns out, all their interfering and "knowing better" discourse came up short. More than being wrong, they actually inserted their "two cents" and attempted to sway the vote to "stay!" How can a "free press" scream about a competing news source's quality yet is comfortable with taking sides in a foreign national matter which had yet to be determined?

The media's bloody nose was richly deserved when Britain quenched its natural yearning and regained her independent sovereignty. And of course, our eventual November tallies would again dwarf their credibility.

As America's campaigning days dwindled, reports of a "decisive" or "landslide" Clinton victory pounded the American voter with a relentless cadence. One personal favorite, from AP's lead writer Julie Pace, perfectly frames what in hindsight qualifies as "fake news" but at the time, was typical of the media's pro Clinton exuberance; Her subsequent headline—POLL: CLINTON APPEARS TO BE ON

CUSP OF BIG WIN—details both her personal expectations and her industry's preference.

However, Pace's writing lacked any factual accounting. Throughout, it was an opinion piece which quoted the statistical findings of an Associated Press poll and was spiced with just one Republican voter's refusal to vote for Trump. While hardly newsworthy, her partiality typifies the media's fall from grace as opinion writers regularly capture front page ink.

This is a journalistic "crap shoot" since opinions are just that and are open to discussion, which is why the editorial page includes "letters to the editor." When in the course of events, those glaring front page opines become undressed, the stature and reputation of the industry suffers.

America's media has knowingly dispersed false info for too long. This has been the case with the public's continuing indoctrination of being a "democracy." If the MSM now objects to "fake news" from internet sources, why this penchant for what is not, never was and hopefully never will be?

After this lengthy season of persuasion, it's obvious that "fake news" failed to alter the election outcome. While it remains distant from any objective analysis, the overall cause of Hillary's second place finish is totally due to Hillary's message, performance and her personal presentation. Suffice to say that her "deplorable" charge, along with promises of freebies verses Trump's concrete pledges deflated her support.

The media's own grab bag of fakery routinely includes distortions, omissions, misquotes, including their partial "taken out of context" usage. Also reliable, is the media's favorite shadowy player, the ever active "anonymous source."

From long ago, the brand of reckless journalism which revises actual events was particularly evident for "Stateside" accounts during the Vietnam War. Ever wonder what caused the American media to uniformly report that the 1968 communist Tet offensive was a huge American defeat, when in fact, it was an over whelming victory? How was it that our "Fourth Estate" failed to publicize North Vietnamese General Giap's belief that all could be lost?

What influenced our media's detour from the truth? Was it really just a matter of personal preference and if so, how does such bias outweigh editing prowess and American sacrifice? So, excuse me for being "put off" by this sudden claim of "fake news" but such fakery, at a much higher and costly level, has been the media's bread and butter for way too long!

Another journalistic misstep is the media's moaning about Clinton's capturing the majority of the votes. Will somebody please inform the publishers/editors/writers/orators click that our system is not a democracy?

In wrapping up their supportive Clinton campaign, their post-election reactions of frustration and embarrassments are long overdue! Just maybe this is the result of their disrespect for the American voter's ability to retain their own thoughts, especially when truth overtakes their hogwash?

With A Gentle Heart

January 19, 2017

Guess what? Donald Trump won the election, but the most important revelation is America dodged a socialist bullet. This is the only valid view for understanding what was prevented. All the hand wringing of republican versus democrat were merely a side show of partisan bickering the true finality of this election was whether America would remain free or eventually become enslaved.

This blunt analysis will not be bandied about on our radio/televised talk circuits. As the back-and-forth politicos' ramble on, their-in-place structures limit the subject matter beforehand. As such, the big "C" will never make it into their filtered talking points.

The same can be said of the dailies which have finally fallen on unfavorable times. The avenues of radio and television have yet to experience the public doubting which has landed upon their printed brethren. This is based probably upon the instantaneousness and personal appeal of talk rather than the finality of print. However, the potential for this seems eventual, given its overall redundant product so stay tuned.

As we gaze about and anticipate Trump's inauguration on the 20th, it would not be an exaggeration to cite the brewing of a calamity. Coming off the shock of the election, the anti-Trump forces flexed their defiant muscles with immediate demonstrations while at the same time, democrat voices were bellowing their highly emotional cries of election thievery.

At the government's hub, dissention later turned to vows of noncompliance and nonattendance by sworn representatives of the American people. Their numbers began with Georgia Congressman, John Lewis, a crusty hallmark from those MLK/Selma days. Roughly a week later, his stance has received approximately sixty fellow representatives.

As this assemblage increases, I am reminded of former Lt. Col. and Congressman Allen West's assessment of the caliber of House members. He estimated that somewhere between 70-80 congressional members were communists or communist leaning. So, expect the Lewis number of no-shows to at least equal those estimated West numbers.

However unsettling as this prospect seems, it dovetails with the progressive college curriculums. This young influx now mans the ranks of a growing anti-Trump army. Concurrent with many campus gatherings is the red meat of drastic financial futures along with the idyllic rhymes of equality. No longer will the rich and affluent dictate. No longer will debt be the calling card at college graduations. Since students will become tomorrow's leaders, their dedicated struggle must join with the working class to better serve humanity for eliminating the discriminatory agenda of a President Trump.

Joining the college idealist is the element of hired protestors, which are now validated from videos of past demonstrations. So, at an event of this nature, with all the pomp and circumstance of a peaceful transfer of government from one leader to another, it should behoove the authorities to possess a working knowledge, an identification list of past hoodlums who masquerade as protestors.

More to the point, what of Trump's message is worthy of such actions? How is it that a highly successful businessman can be painted with a gender/racial discriminatory brush, when in fact his multi blend of employees states otherwise?

Is securing our nation's border so discriminatory or is it a logical cure to the darker element that arrives illegally? And since when did undocumented Middle Easterners become such valued assets? Especially when they arrive without any verification of beneficial worth? And what's so threatening when eliminating the hundreds of billions of wasted tax dollars spent upon governmental regulations which generally hamper growth and stymies productivity?

Then there's the global warming/climate change hysteria. Remember the eruption from Mount St Helens? Darken skies, only to evaporate within the earth's atmosphere? It's OK to be concerned but balance that emotion with some factual data, not with some fanciful prediction such as Gore's doomsday talk about "ice-free Arctic summers by 2013."

Trump came out of nowhere to take charge on a stage full of politicians who would only venture replies for the delight of the voters. Trump's frank talk was by contrast, unmistakable and at the same time what has been missing and longed for by our American people for too long.

During the campaign season, Trump's opponent lacked any worthwhile messaging. Her preference was to only besmirch and criticize. That along with the lopsided rally numbers and Obamacare's final hammer of increased premiums sealed her loss.

In conclusion, I pray for my Country, my next President, for fair weather and gentle hearts. However, with the knowledge of the communist mind, tactics and their apparent youthful attraction, this Presidential term is an opportunity not to be wasted. God Bless America!

PRESIDENT DONALD J. TRUMP

Misinformation Personified

March 16, 2017

On the surface, the fallacy that "America is a democracy" seems to be a case of "no big deal," yet, given its drastic reality with today's sad acceptance, the opposite is not only true, but its critical difference must be realized. Ever wonder as to how this misunderstanding of one's government became so accepted?

Why is it that government, academia and our media people continue with its promotion of this falsehood? Such a consistency reflects an intended purpose! Do not be fooled into thinking this is a mere trifle since it attacks the very core of our governing, our unity and our American heritage. And yes, its institutionalized and insistent promotion seems to threaten.

Democracy operates chiefly upon majority rule. I mention this in conjunction with the recent cries that Clinton actually won the election based upon the "popular vote." If America was a democracy, Clinton would be President. Thanks to our Founders, popular vote totals are irrelevant!

Breaking it down into finer parts, America's presidential election is composed of fifty separate State elections. Within this Federalist system, each State records their votes through their number of electors which are determined from their representative numbers in Congress.

This system of separate State elections further discounts the myth that America is a democracy, yet each generation is taught this fallacy. Driven by the losses of Gore and now Clinton, too many Americans believe that not awarding the Presidency to the one with the most votes is cheating.

So, with this recent Clinton example, what resides in fantasy world now screams for more detailing. In part, we are pounded daily about this "fake news" product in addition to school curriculums espousing this false democracy dynamic without any push back! In reality, this now persists simply because of its lengthy tenure which likewise molded previous generations, so at this point, who knows any difference?

The above-cited question of "why" requires substance. A review of our Forefathers opinions discarded democracy as being preposterous and dangerous. Quotes abound. John Adams stated, "There never was a democracy yet that did not commit suicide" while in agreement, James Madison said, "Democracies have ever been spectacles of turbulence and contention…been as short in their lives as they have been violent in their deaths." Fisher Ames concurred with, "A democracy is a volcano which conceals the fiery materials of its own destruction." And Noah Webster believed that "…a pure democracy is generally a very bad government. It is often the most tyrannical government on earth."

One last quote, from English statesman G.K. Chesterton tends to examine democracy's underbelly with his words; "You can never have a revolution in order to establish a democracy. You must have a democracy in order to have a revolution." So given this universal aversion, why would we now embrace such a knowing tragedy? Or is tragedy the ultimate goal?

Consider how misled those are who believe that Hillary Clinton was short changed, or the notion of an unjust judicial finding versus Gore. The common culprit leading them down this road of discontent and malice of thought is this continual voicing, at every authoritative level, that America is a democracy.

Such belief is also the result from the lesson plans which our youthful minds were force fed. Accordingly, the adult voters who continue to grumble four months after the election are merely responding to a lifetime of misguided info. If only for peace of mind, isn't it time for truth?

With our Founders denunciations, there shouldn't be any doubt as to why our government is structured as a Constitutional Republic rather than being a mob scene. In a Republic, citizens elect their own individual representatives who, being directly answerable to their vote, enact the laws which govern and ultimately affect their States. Therefore, the frequent emotional input from democracy's loud majority is erased through the people's duly elected representatives.

Despite all those earlier warnings, and in conjunction with the abundance of opportunities afforded from our present structure of governing, the question still remains; why? Why this penchant, this universal chorus if not to lay the foundation for supporting change?

And with that word "change" a more sinister memory lingers. America just barely survived eight years of a Presidential administration which had as its clarion call, fundamental change; or more precisely, from a President Elect announcing prior to his Inauguration Day, "We are five days away from fundamentally transforming the United States of America."

Enough Americans embraced this suicidal call for fundamental change that one had to not only fear such radicalism but also wonder just what was so pressing or so terrible as to validate this foundational redoing. At the same time, for those who know better, it became clear that this misstep in basic citizenship was and is a haven for breeding discontent and "fundamental" change!

In retrospect, that question of "why" has been answered most ominously. An immediate return of Civics to our nation's classrooms must be, if only to ensure ourselves an orderly and peaceful American future!

Common Sense Thinking

March 27, 2017

The February 1st headline announced, "Democrats force delays in votes on 3 nominees." Is it just me or is this meant to generate a round of applause? I mean, great, let's clog up our governing. Such negativity would never be the subject of media ink four or eights years ago. These congratulatory headlines are engendered solely upon our citizen President.

While that February announcement still prevails, a March 24th headline again informs, "Dems threaten delay on Gorsuch." Let me see, two months after President Trump's inauguration, democrats are still bruising over the election results? Only this time, the roadblock is against his Supreme Court pick.

Since all who are elected to Congress do so with the public's trust and faith, and with an abidance to both their Constitutional dictates and sworn loyalty by oath to serve their constituents and Country alike, one must wonder as to what or who is being served by this platform of negative, even combative conduct? Concerning this Supreme Court nomination, just what is so repugnant about Neil Gorsuch's jurisprudence, other than his Constitutional adherence? Consequently, what is so repugnant about our Constitution?

Within this Gorsuch report, I find it very telling that of the six democrat Senators to be quoted in this AP report, even including one who is "open to voting for him" (Gorsuch), the writer wisely omits the name of a fellow Senate interrogator who is somewhat iffy, based upon his past conduct.

Explain how Democrat Sen. Richard Blumenthal, Connecticut, managed to weasel his way onto this "hang 'em high" kangaroo panel? I mean, being elected as a Senator already reflected badly upon his constituents but to actually level judgment over such a highly placed judicial appointee seems offensive. If nothing else, his presence turns back the pages to another Supreme Court inquisitor with a murky past; that of the "Lion of the Senate," Ted Kennedy, with his Bork hearing escapades

A more accurate portrait of this Senator, from the pen of columnist Kathleen Parker's March 24th piece questions; "How does a man who embellishes his military career – implying that he fought in Vietnam when, in fact he received five deferments before serving stateside – consider himself worthy to prosecute the qualifications of one of the nation's most brilliant jurists?" He then, in 2010, attempted to weasel out of his lie by inferring that he only meant that he was in the service during that time of war.

Then consider this current tale; Gorsuch will guarantee a conservative Court majority. He, by replacing conservative icon Antonin Scalia, only resets the previous make up, of which was seated when Obamacare was upheld. This is another false notion which has been bandied about routinely.

Honestly, what irritates the Schumers of this world is that Gorsuch represents a Constitutional originalism, ala the Scalia mold. And given his youth, his Constitutional influence will continue for decades.

The present age of the Court sends shivers through the democrat ranks. This reasoning was what moved Obama to select Judge Garland. If Obama's pick was approved, Garland would have cemented a liberal majority by turning the most notable conservative robe inside out.

Throughout this confirmation process, the gotcha attempts which make up the line of questioning are equally shabby. Pennsylvania Democrat Sen. Casey cited his concerns over Gorsuch's "rigid and restrictive judicial philosophy." Obviously, his rigidity negates any progressive altering from their "living Constitution" theorems or individual re-interpretations.

While Casey's comment had to do with political preference, other inquiries attempted to corner the appointee concerning the infamous Roe v. Wade decision. These petulantly childish tactics reflect badly upon a judiciary which endures the public's questioning of what their Roe v. Wade finding so rightly generates.

What's With an Oath?

October 5, 2017

It is obvious that even in our President's own Republican Party; there are those that are disgruntled by the election results. But what causes such discontent from within the winning party? Our first President, George Washington cautioned against the "spirit of the party." Of course, his time was way too soon to warn of the woes from "the establishment" and its hierarchy but both influences originate from the same kettle.

What is being permitted and supported with bi-partisan support, most notably with this deafening republican silence, is this Mueller led investigation into what hasn't even been discovered. This, in combination with media efforts to falsely accuse with "gotcha" styled journalism, has superseded the normality of any proper investigation.

Previously, evidence of a possible crime required "probable cause" so that warrants, and other investigative tools could be employed. Now, with this former FBI paragon of virtue charging away, all such essentials have been ignored since in the end, this political vendetta to discredit and hopefully rid Washington of a Presidential outsider is what it's all about! And all the while, Trump's supposed loyal Republican cast remains tongue tied or partially obliging.

However, members from both sides of the political spectrum take an oath of office. And it is for this that they should be held accountable. Now refresh with the following.

All those federally elected take this oath of office: "Do you solemnly swear that you will support and defend the Constitution of the United States against all enemies, foreign and domestic; that you will bear true faith and allegiance to the same; that you take this obligation freely, without any mental reservation or purpose of evasion; and that you will well and faithfully discharge the duties of the office on which you are about to enter: So help you God?" Their answer is "I do." Those last four words were added to the original inaugural oath by George Washington in 1789.

What recourse do we have when electing a public servant which reneges on his or her sworn duties? Accountability to one's office and to those ones represents is enshrined within one's sworn oath. Without adherence to one's word, all else is lost as now is the case too often.

This is what is happening in Congress today and I for one am sick and tired of this Congressional stalemate based upon revenge. Consider the facts from a Wall Street Journal editorial, "Mr. Trump has made 18 nominations to appellate courts, 39 to district courts and three to the U.S. Federal Claims. The Senate has confirmed only four for the appellate courts."

This has gotten to the point of just refusing to perform one's obligated duties. Such blatant defiance echoes thoughts of disloyalty while staining both the public's trust and diminishing the effectiveness of our federal authority. As such, this refusal to perform, or if you will, this silent rebellion, against official duties etched within one's oath must be addressed as directed by and for the support of our Constitution.

We as a free people expect a different result, one that at least serves if not enhances our Country and her citizens. If not addressed and improved, the American voter, you know, that "necessary" every other year "evil," could and should embark upon a massive re-election effort, solely based upon ridding personal disloyalty from our Congressional ranks.

Obviously, the most crucial element in this undertaking is the search for the highest character qualities in those selected. However, as Trump has so clearly illustrated, our quest may be best served by skipping over those holding political science degrees or who have risen from the lower rungs of either party. In fact, it might be advisable to center our search onto those who have demonstrated an ability to work and succeed in the private sector, since by their pursuits, things do get accomplished!

Can't Avoid It

October 12, 2017

Try as I might, there's just no getting away from those three little letters, CFR! From some of my previous pieces, readers are familiar with the alphabet version for the Council on Foreign Relations. So, this morning's print tightened my britches just a wee bit when reading two vastly diverse accounts, from two different publications. Still, both were tied at the hip with those three letters.

One account, entitled, "Dems who opposed Iran nuke deal urge Trump to keep pact," drew my interest immediately. This AP piece concerned the switching of one's previous vote from being against the Iranian nuclear deal, supposedly because Trump is President. Of course, with current political feathers still flying on both sides of the aisle from that November shocker, this on again-off again allegiance is to be expected, as the Obamacare back and forth has shockingly taught us.

However, what caught my attention was the unmasking of those charged with making that disastrous Iran deal in the first place! First and foremost, Mr. John Kerry, Sec. of State, followed by Mr. Ernest Moniz, Energy Secretary and finally, Ms. Wendy Sherman, Undersecretary of State for political affairs. This account detailed how these three met with European ambassadors "behind closed doors."

Talk about a fixed deal? All three were and are CFR members. Not only that, one of the representatives cited in the article with changing his vote, Representative Eliot Engel, Democrat New York, is also a CFR member.

Meanwhile, a Wall Street Journal article, U.S. Sets Goal: Dilute NAFTA informs about both our President's insistence to renegotiate this lopsided NAFTA deal and those who would balk at such a revision.

One anti-revisionist is none other than Mr. Thomas Donohue, president of the U.S. Chamber of Commerce. Need I also cite his CFR credentials? He is quoted saying, "We've reached a critical moment." Also, the article describes Mr. Donohue's position as "fighting his own government's plans."

Donohue's position is aided by Trump's own U.S. Trade Representative Robert Lighthizer, who again is another like minded CFR guy who tried to be positive with his brief quote of "have made good progress."

Not to depress but even the stoutest doubter must wonder about just who or what interest is steering America's past and current policies and of course why Trump's shocking victory upsets more that just our Congressional thin skins!

These two humongous deals have one thing in common, the shafting of America! Also identified within these two accounts are those doing the shafting. All I managed to do was to connect the dots to the globalist organization which directs them!

Consider the dominance within these two ongoing issues. America's total representation at the Iran Nuclear deal and those currently against a commonsense revision of a one-sided trade pact are all CFR! Is it any wonder that the only spokesman for America is the outsider, our President?

Much needs to change in Washington but it must start with the average non-elitist becoming the people's elected representative. This is the only assurance for avoiding this entrenched and dominating influence. The CFR's voice and its agenda has saturated all field of endeavors.

America's charted slide has been halted by an outsider who owes no one a penny! He only cares about and loves his Country. Is he rambunctious with his remarks and tweets? Seems that way, but Mom always said that "the truth hurts." And the truth is that the vast majority of Americans are unaware of the CFR's existence, let alone its everyday influence and control. That in itself, should alarm us into a jealous defense of all that we have been Blessed with and to give thanks for a truly pro-American President!

All Too Obvious

November 10, 2017

Consistency speaks for itself. All of a sudden, ala Herman Cain from years past, another threat is rearing its mighty presence as Judge Roy Moore is seen as possibly another Trumper in the Senate.

Remember the 2012 Presidential elections when Mr. Cain presented a challenge to both Obama's minority Presidency and his hold on the black voting block? Then, after leading in the Republican polls, claims of sexual harassment eventually caused his withdrawal despite his denial of any wrongdoing. Following his departure, it was odd that nothing more was ever heard from the accuser or of those supposed charges.

Judge Roy Moore will be a Senate presence which the establishment would rather not have to deal with. In this era when Christianity is at least being questioned, as in America being a Christian Nation and as next month's greeting of "Merry Christmas" will again generate frowns, Roy Moore's probable December victory, along with his deeply rooted Christian beliefs represents an unnecessary obstacle to both sides of the aisle.

Now, after close to forty years, candidate Moore has been accused of having sexual contact with a minor. Also, in the same general time span, three other women now sudden remember similar encounters with the then assistant District Attorney. Obviously, Roy Moore denies any wrongdoing.

Why didn't Moore's negative publicity stir the memories of his accusers when he was removed as Alabama's Chief Supreme Court

Justice? Another instance was after being voted back into his Chief Justice position, he refused to obey a U.S. Supreme Court order which legalized gay marriages; he was again dismissed from the bench. Again, dismissed yet still, not a whimper was heard from his supposed victims!

Trump's arrival provides reason enough why another outsider will not be tolerated. On the legislative venue, our President has been stymied simply based upon his upstaging of their established political brethren. An outsider slipped in and now must be humiliated and made impotent.

Aside from politics, there is also the religious angle. The Judge is more than a Christian since his record and past actions are faith based and inspirational within his Alabama venue. So, enlarging Moore's stage would give him more of an audience and greater exposure.

The naysayers may object but given the cold reception which our Christmas holiday now receives, who can argue against this so-called "war against Christianity? Hell, we just finished with a twice elected President who voiced his belief about "America isn't a Christian nation." Then there is Tim Tebow! Here is a quarterback who played in the NFL playoffs, yet who remains essentially barred from the league?

Also too, here is a man, Roy Moore, who has amassed a lifetime of admirable service. A West Point graduate and Vietnam veteran, he reflects a hard working, horse back riding, down to earth candidate who is a deeply religious and is a devoted family man.

The bottom line to all this tabloid gossip is that since Trump's arrival, the media has emerged as not only being biased, but it also now airs and/or prints unsubstantiated articles with complete disregard. In fact, this was the subject of Wall Street Journal's Kimberly A. Strassel's recent piece entitled, "Lifting the Steele Curtain."

For many, the media has done themselves in. How can anyone believe that what they read or hear is fact when Ms. Strassel, along with similar Fox News reporting, points out that, "Fusion GPS dossiers was one of the dirtiest political tricks in U.S. history." In part, Ms. Strassel continues with, "This dossier allegation is ludicrous on its face...Yet the press ran with it."

And now, with or without any substantiating, today's media hears of a juicy report which could aid in the disembarking of a probable

Senate winner, one who will support Trump at every turn. And "the press ran with it?"

Even the reported details, not of an adult woman but a vulnerable minor, then re-enforced by not one or two but three additional reports of lesser action and intent stretch the laws of probability. After decades of being in the public venue, this mystical affair doesn't jive with Moore's solid record of faith, service and family. And then, when Sen. McCain jumps at the chance to offer that Moore must drop out of the race regardless, this becomes a package too conveniently wrapped!

Why This Pentagon

December 12, 2017

Let me get this headline straight; "transgender people can enlist in military Jan 1." One question, where is the need and is our military that short of warm bodies? OK, so it's a multiple question but you get the idea! We get it but what about that useless Pentagon?

I defy anyone to name a "need," or to explain the reasoning, not from a feel-good social engineering perspective but from a military point of view. And equally absent, if there are numbers needed, there's always the draft! Heaven forbids but those that answered the call did so in fine and admirable fashion.

But returning to that excrement center, the Pentagon, where was their input when American trade was aiding North Vietnam? Military commanders in the field, not at the Pentagon but in the boonies, also stated that the war could be won in six weeks or so if the restrictions over our troops were lifted. Why didn't the Pentagon overrule McNamara as they are now?

More to the point in August 1966, quoting State Dept. publication 8117, "All American citizens should know that any American businessman who chooses to engage in peaceful trade with the Soviet Union or Eastern European countries and to sell the goods he buys is acting within his rights and is following the policy of his government."

This despicable publication adds that, "any organization, however patriotic in intention, that undertakes to boycott, blacklist, or otherwise penalize or attack any American business for engaging in peaceful trade with eastern European countries or the Soviet Union, is acting against the interests of the United States."

So, with this bit of authorized treason, is it any surprise as to the Pentagon's wacky attempt to weaken troop morale and combat efficiency with this inclusion of transgenders into our military ranks?

Now if this isn't bad enough, how about Peter Arnett's interview of Secretary of State Dean Rusk when he was incredibly asked if our government provided the North Vietnamese the bombing targets for the next day? Rusk answered in the positive since it was feared that innocent people would otherwise be killed. To add further, from personal experience, the order of the day was not to fire until fired upon, for the same concern, civilian deaths or what we called today, "collateral damage."

All this points to why ISIS is now no more. We have a President who expects our Generals to general. The ROE's (rules of engagement) have been lifted with positive results. These results are telling and in retrospect, Vietnam should have been a victory.

The reasoning for transgenders in our military is equally as asinine as were those former ROE's. Also, it is counterproductive and expensive. Such policies reflect upon another ROE which forbade our pilots from bombing SAM missile sights that were under construction. They were only legitimate targets if they were operational. Again, the "first fired upon" policy.

All this magnifies the bloated and often counterproductive state of our federal governing. This insubordinate Pentagon is something out of "the old wild west!" If nothing else, the military has a "chain of command" of which the President retains command. Civilian courts are hardly the answer. This goes to the heart of command and to strictness of order.

Supposedly, the Pentagon has instituted the stiffest of requirements for the entry of transgenders. Consider one such stipulation: "if a medical provider certifies they've been clinically stable in the preferred sex for 18 months."

Plainly visible is the Pentagon's concern for appearing politically correct! We are not talking about the required stability for being a bank teller or cashier at the supermarket. This is the damn military! Combat is not dictated by clean and/or safe working conditions or by a union contract!

To think that the Pentagon consists of senior officers who operate and formulate decisions gained from their extensive military experience; for this finding, after a six-month review period, is so ludicrous that all those involved should be immediately reassigned, retired or even terminated.

As a matter of fact, given the success of those generals in the field, just what is the Pentagon's purpose if not political? And after such a lengthy and disastrous following of those ROE's, of which the Pentagon remained silent, if I remember correctly, it all comes down to, why this Pentagon?

Its Cornerstone is Omission

December 30, 2017

Throughout this whirlwind, known as the Trump candidacy and eventual election, what has continued unscathed through it all is the most secretive and influential of organizations. Its use of omission has concealed a conspiratorial effort never before imagined in both its efficiency and duration.

This shadowy existence is now approaching its century mark yet only a miniscule number of Americans are even aware of its existence. So with this, time has come to unveil this dastardly Council on Foreign Relations, or simply the CFR.

During America's modern era, generally since World War II, our government has sadly come under the CFR's agenda and influence. In remarkable fashion, the Wall Street Journal (WSJ) recently featured two seemingly innocent articles; one detailing the list of possible candidates for the Federal Reserve Boards while the second mimicked this anti Trump chorus concerning our new tax law.

In the first piece entitled, Economists Considered for High-Level Fed Post, photos of two candidates, one double in size and smiling intended to sway readers since the smaller photo featured a sterner facial expression.

I mention what seems like an innocuous slight simply to point out the details to which this secretive cabal seizes upon for gaining even the slightest of public sentiment. The larger photo of the grinning candidate is that of an unknown CFR member while the other represents a threat to their control of what was created over one hundred years ago, the illegal Federal Reserve!

Within this article, in addition to the smiling Richard Clarida, no less than three other CFR members were cited. Most critical was the changing of the CFR guard from Chairwoman Janet Yellen to the incoming Chairman Jerome Powell. Funny how that works, isn't it? Also named was "only one other PhD. Economist, Lael Brainard."

Trump's election presented a helter-skelter effect upon this globalist group since Hillary was an obliging CFR tool and has publicly likened the CFR to being her "mothership." So, the Trump Presidency not only inserted a hitch to the CFR's global get along, but it also generated a fear that a resurgence of economic strength will accompany Trump's corporate tax deductions. This must be averted as socialism best works with the needy and dependent.

Now onto the second WSJ piece entitled, Almost Everything Is Wrong with the New Tax Law, written by Alan S. Blinder, another CFR spokesman who also was "a former vice chairman of the Federal Reserve." Funny how all this ties together, isn't it?

Funny maybe, however all this slips under the public's radar screen since most Americans remain in the dark as to its sinister existence and free wheeling operational influence.

Mr. Blinder details four tax bill items, which he condemns severely with, "that Americans hate this bill. And they should." Forget the first three since they re-enforced the usual media bias. However, it's the fourth point that pertains to the globalist's (CFR) holy grail.

To quote Blinder, "Fourth, a Congress truly focused on tax reform would not have thrust a completely unrelated dagger into the heart of Obamacare." While this supposedly was Obama's main claim for his legacy, it also marked a major socialized shift in America. Blinder and the CFR's concern, in addition to a lowered tax base, was their setback by Trump's back door anti-Obamacare effort, which should shortly become history!

The point to all this CFR skullduggery is that ever since it's 1921 creation, America has undergone a slow but unrelenting transformation which has caused a weakening of her former self; even our bright spot of a WWII victory opened America up to a disaster; one that had previously been anticipated, designed and formulated by the CFR's cadre. One only has to gaze at their monstrous creation in New York City, the United Nations, for our understanding of their evil intent.

America has been handed a reprieve which we now all sense. The WSJ articles, when properly realized, represent an accurate portrayal of the CFR's tactics for steering both public opinion and monetary control. Without our awareness and subsequent push back, it will continue to dictate our headlines and direct our Country's future.

Americans Taking Stock

January 8, 2018

The need to realize this negative flow which has entered our modern-day version of America's society is the most necessary and beneficial undertakings which await us all. It's called, "taking stock," both individually and totally as proud Americans. The fact that this remains waiting points to its pressing need!

Why is this? Simply because there is an ongoing agenda to circumvent any of America's fundamentals; the studying of ageless principles such as America's Founding, her faith-based heritage and Constitutional structure, personal individualism, morality and National loyalty. Without these foundational pillars of guidance and knowledge, we are merely dupes who dangle upon the directive words of authority.

Has anyone attempted to digest fully the breath of negativity which spurns continuously from an industry which previously was heralded as being a free press? In all likelihood, that former identity is now considered a relic, but have we ever wondered when this attitude took hold? Are we even capable of pondering why we cavalierly toss away what our Founders valued so highly? How many would even ask, "Who are Founders?" With this changing attitude, dare we question what spurs this American floundering?

These queries pertain to the condition which has transpired from our slow and methodical transformation when being mentally steered. And in a free society, this state is verboten since the devious always take advantage of the manipulated. Think about the end result from this instituted ignorance. What is the difference between one who can't read versus one who won't?

Without getting too specific, the media's general reaction since November 2016, mainly pivots upon its false narrative. This rash of unsubstantiated Trump headlines would be comical if our people had a normal sense of the traditional standards and principles which have been academically trashed.

Conversely, this symmetry between a weaken course study and the equally affected public word introduces an unnoticeable creeping of a designed mischief against our American fiber. The final product or destination of both crippling effects is one thing, but the overall intent is something which needs to be reversed.

Looking back, there was a time when communism was not embedded within America's trading partners but represented our number one enemy. The very fact that all this has morphed into a "see no evil" commerce standard should be mind boggling when remembering the forgotten or just ignored "Red" in what was "Red China."

Once again, who benefits? Certainly not the American consumer. Those cheap overseas manufacturing prices have slowly crept upwards while its iffy craftsmanship continues to sink. This trading deception also needs reviewing yet due to our current mental malaise, we routinely object to Trump's proper and timely trading revisions. Again, without that foundation of American understanding, which includes a basic appreciation for loyalty, including its proper "America first" priorities, that "see no evil" sentiment will prevail without any hint of its deceptive practices.

And lastly, the limitless assaults against that November election shocker has elevated the media's liberal bias into the lofty perches of intentional deception and lying at will. Their flaunting of arrogance, which never before editorialized with such boldness, is emblematic of a dark future; if the public's inherent duty of recognition and subsequent "push back" continues in absentia. What is needed is a people pause to reflect upon the idea of what is so damn harmful of America being first?

If truth can once again be valued, it will reveal that instead of a free and sovereign people's "push back," today's 'push back" has come from the "establishment's" defying of a legitimately elected President; simply because he represents an interruption to their design for America's gradual decent into socialism. Instead, Trump brings a return to a patriotic elevation and the cherishing of an America and her rightful status which was, and which needs to be again. America's foundations need and hopefully will be revitalized but first, she is searching for a proper recognition and appreciation from her own people.

Trump Versus the Global Scheme

January 10, 2018

The "word on the street" is that Trump's speech to America's farmers was another gem. At this point, what else to expect from this non-politician who with each passing day, seems more adapting and self assured. Part of his allure and charm is the remembrance of a 2012 Romney cave in compared to a man who relishes not only a challenge but most certainly playing the part of both the instigator and counterpuncher.

Is it any wonder why America's pampered "establishment" is so tense and unnerved? As such, the media's daily charge amounts to desperation from its fits of frustration. Never before has a conservative been so brash and undaunted. While each Mueller charge momentarily strengthens the media's gusto, when the verbal dust clears, Trump remains standing.

Issues deemed critical for preserving garner the most media attention and subsequent ink. Set apart through an extensive coverage, these establishment pet issues raise the rhetoric bar and thus become a crusade issue by comparison. This was the case when through their NAFTA prism, evaluating Trump's Tennessee speech to the farming industry took on a dire consequence. Hyped throughout the ensuing commentary were the references to their sacred NAFTA agreement. How dare Trump even mention disengagement!

Forgive my inquisitive nature but how did American farmers manage before NAFTA? I recall that there were seasons for buying and likewise "out of seasons" for not. I also recall that California was and probably still is famous for their avocado industry. So, what is it with the importation of these Mexican avocados? Other than not growing that delicious fruit altogether, which I highly doubt, what is the destination for those California avocados?

How about this brainstorm, instead of importing what we grow domestically, why not just stop exporting and sell American produce to the American consumer? What a novel concept! Are we to believe that since the creation of NAFTA, Americans are destined to consume foreign grown produce? If so, tell me again just how critical this NAFTA treachery is!

Trump's talk to the farmers was a refreshingly American styled presentation complete with his acknowledgement that "Farm country is God's country." Talk about connecting and being with people! This is in opposition to secularism which is globally promoted. Since our Christmas observances are still fresh, there is little doubt as to the ongoing assault against Christianity, yet this "happy holidays" ruse debate must wait for another time.

Very telling is a Wall Street Journal's (WSJ) commentary entitled Will Trump Punish the Farm Belt? Obviously, this source considers it beneficial to maintain the current status quo surrounding this issue as it inserts a dose of fear and insecurity to our possible NAFTA withdrawal. Also too, they just can't get past Trump's immediate exiting from that Tran-Pacific Partnership, TPP, which contrary to its spin, would have severely crippled America's independent sovereignty!

Within this NAFTA piece, the WSJ informed, "Mr. Trump already walloped U.S. farm exporters when he dropped out of the Trans-Pacific Partnership." Further into this pro-NAFTA article, I have caught a glimpse of where my avocados went when reading, "The U.S. sends about $18 billion a year in farm products to Mexico and $23 billion to Canada, which together accounts for a third of American farm exports." Simple math suggests that our farmers export $123 billion worth of produce annually. Shouldn't such an outpouring put a dent into third world hunger? Forgive the attempt at humor, it hardly suffices for such a counter productive and mindless policy.

Finally, given that the American consumer is now relegated to the back of the consumer pack, we need to return to the Trump basics of America being first. We need, as our President has exemplified, to extricate ourselves from these un-American trade entanglements. The American consumer should have first dibs on what America grows in her own soil and not be fed the produce from third world fields. This is outrageous!

Is America Still Deserving?

June 4, 2018

The heart of any nation is its life, along with its protection and enjoyment. In America, we are guided with the words from our Pledge, "under God." Yet for too long, many Americans have not only condoned a most injurious blasphemy, but also vehemently defended and protected its venue.

Responding to recently passed and signed legislation barring legal abortions after the detection of a heartbeat, a temporary injunction was ordered, which from any logical interpretation of Constitutional Law, must be viewed as an intentional act of inhumanity, along with it being unconstitutional. Sadly, this ruling also lengthens America's distance from her original sense of decency, human kindness and her absolutes of right and wrong.

Have we not lost our way? Has life become too cumbersome and restrictive, too demanding? Will our material glitz and clutter only remain as evidence of our existence? What matters if not life, and if not for the preciousness of life, what have we become?

Billed as "the most restrictive abortion law in the country," this decision from Iowa's Judge Michael Huppert delays the law's final implementation for months! Its push back came from the usual suspects: the ACLU of Iowa, Planned Parenthood and the Emma Goldman Clinic; all of which claimed that banning abortions based upon detecting a fetal heartbeat "is unconstitutional."

Are we crazy? Ok, Roe v Wade was interpreted as law in 1973 and since then, estimates inform that well over 53 million abortions have been performed. I would suggest to those plaintiffs in Iowa's "heartbeat abortion" case that this grotesque total of lives lost is not only a blatant violation of constitutional law, but it itemizes the dearest of costs for our comforted indifference while highlighting today's amoral nature.

More to the point, just what is unconstitutional with using a heartbeat as the ultimate decider of life or death? Is it not the starting point when administering aid in emergency situations? Also, how is it logical to protest the finality facing death row inmates while vehemently defending those seeking to abort?

Also, too, consider the era when Roe v. Wade somehow gained constitutional muster. Vietnam was finally being laid to rest after years of weekly casualty totals and often grisly nighttime viewing. Could that drumbeat of war and death be a possible numbing or conditioning prior to passing Roe v. Wade?

Who remembers the Supreme Court's McCollum v. Board of Education case of 1948 which found that religious instruction in schools was unconstitutional? This whimsical decision should have casted doubt upon our assumptions of infallibility for nine black robes?

Then another judicial faux pas came with the more recent Obamacare trespass. This decision somehow fathomed that American citizens must pay for a product that was, in most cases, neither wanted nor affordable. That or be fined! These outcomes bolster the probability that even judiciaries may enter into an outlaw state when the Constitutional oversight from Congress is not enforced. Recognition of this lack may have provided additional impetus for entering that unconstitutional realm of its Roe v. Wade finding!

Consider our wayward direction from when America's Founding was based on unimpeded religious freedoms for all denominations and faiths. Embedded within all beliefs was the sanctity of life. So, with the public's complicity in full view since 1973, is there any wonder as to why today's anti-Christian crusade continues to bellow?

Through recent years, we have extended far beyond our normal claim of freedom. All freedom co-exists with responsibility and accountability. As such, abortion is an after-the-fact decision to what was not necessarily, in many instances, a responsible act. Interestingly, its demand is compounded through this opposition against the teaching of abstinence, which in turn only heightens the irresponsibility of it all.

Contrary to the anti-life dogma being echoed by our judiciary, the "fundamental right to have a safe and legal abortion" is a fallacy since only Congress legislates and enacts law, not nine over-the-top justices. Therefore, this "law of the land" refrain is mainly employed to instill compliance based upon ignorance which begets further judicial banditry.

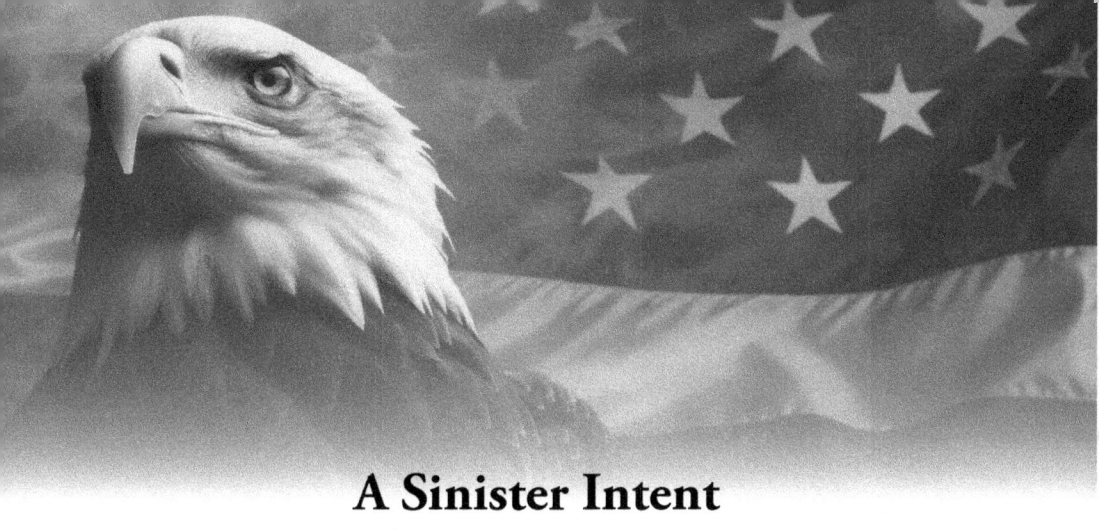

A Sinister Intent

June 18, 2018

Claiming a propaganda outlet as 'the media' or 'the press' only masks what was once a proud profession while protecting its current misdeeds of distortions and fables. If the term 'sinister' seems brutish, what else is more appropriate for an industry which masquerades its intentional false stories as being truthful news reporting?

This age of information has become so suffocating with its totality that avoiding its influence is as nearly impossible as is the stiffening of our resolve against its propagandizing. So, labeling its daily product and overall purpose as 'sinister' is necessary when focusing upon its end game.

Take for instance one's basic ambition to strive and attain success or just being 'successful.' This elementary goal is now downplayed, as media accounts repeatedly prefer tales of 'victimhood' for attracting the public's fancy. This promoting of the abnormal, the crippling, while not singularly rooted in written form, leads to lowering of one's confidence and initiative.

At its highest pinnacle, success must be national as it ultimately touches all lives. Today, nothing underscores this abnormal shift more than the media's treatment of a President. As quickly as the next sunrise, Presidential adoration vanished as shock gave way to bitterness and vitriol following Trump's 2016 election. Excepting one major outlet, this about face became institutionalized throughout as each ordinary instance or innocuous comment became dissected, twisted or exaggerated for the stirring up of public animosity. Appointments and policies received harsher treatment.

Headlines about the absurd, the meaningless and minutest of Presidential flubs were recently featured with the "news" of our President "tearing up White House documents and papers." Apparently, this habit translates into "absolutely breaking the law."

Not treated as inconsequential nor meaning to minimize the value of proper Presidential documentations, this report does reveal the depth to which the media's microscope now inspects verses pre-Trump times. As such, there is an obvious chasm of accounting between then and now. Being new to this political venue, what appears to be a personal and innocent habit from his business days has now caused a media uproar over an injury to what is valued as maintaining the "complete accounting of history."

Were headlines so focused upon these "accounting" concerns, or even to the accounting itself, of that deadly Benghazi night. Not only does an accounting still await, few venture a reason or even a guess about where the President was when that middle of the night call went unanswered. Now, all of a sudden, this "complete accounting," not about details of life and death, but of preserving irrelevant paperwork for posterity becomes a must?

Another example is this over played investigation into what was supposedly Russian collusion but now has drifted into the obstruction of justice arena. This circus should test the public's common sense and patience. While the press decries our President for his tweets about a 'witch hunt,' what term better describes a year plus investigation based upon a 'must be' theory?

The fact that this $20 million plus Mueller effort originated without probable cause, much less evidence, yet manages to still capture front page ink, is an indictment encompassing more than just the media's complicity.

Our President's firm North Korean stand, which was a one eighty from his predecessor, produced a never before meeting with that country's leader. Given that the prospect of a probable nuclear war was stalled and maybe eliminated, our media preferred painting the entire affair with a negative brush while ignoring that the population of South Korea's capital is more than triple that of New York City! As

President Trump said, with such numbers hanging in the balance, he would go anywhere for a meeting.

Once again, 'sinister' is the appropriate word for an industry which ignores American success simply because of one person's deal making tenacity. The media's feeble depictions of frank discussions as being rude is a non- essential versus a rising stock market, record low unemployment and America's growing respect worldwide. So, as the media's emphasis upon untruths and gross distortions continues as does its ignoring of America's return to greatness, the word 'sinister' is relevant and very applicable!

Bottom line is that yes, President Trump differs greatly, but our Country and her citizens are benefiting from his outspoken brand of leadership. Success and its results still matter and President Trump is driven by both!

Education as a Weapon

October 31, 2018

In this land of the free, our future may well be determined by our foolish trusting. Within this confused state, there exists two elements; one is the opportunist, the taker, our enemy while the other is our believing, trusting average American. While diverse in every aspect, with one aware while the other is not, both own actions or non-actions which effectively weaken our independent sovereignty as a Constitutional Republic.

As the title suggests, our need for education has been transformed into a perverse weapon. What this revolves around is the disarming of America's younger minds for their future compliance and support. This approach, in terms of numbers, provides a force in waiting while also detracting from our greatest and most feared strength, a united "we the people."

Consider that the opportunist manipulates, revises or eliminates certain valued and proven lessons while the believer usually adjusts accordingly. Also too, the more truthful may shy away from spreading its valued word, simply from the usual onslaught of insults and recriminations. The truth is most powerful and these tactics prove it!

The media delights with its reporting of Trump's travel ban being nixed; particularly enforced by the Ninth Circuit Court. Without realizing, this media intensity forms an air of intimidation against any proper recourse and is designed for that exact purpose. "Why" you ask? Simply put, media elites know that the Ninth Circuit rulings, with their latest decree being no exception, rest upon legal eggshells.

Congress has the authority to address this obvious hike in judicial activism since under their purview and in full compliance with our Constitution, Congress created all the lower federal courts. So, in one fell swoop, the Ninth and others could undergo a very legal reorganization, reduction or even elimination.

This one example of applying one's Constitutional knowing is the reason which nullifies its classroom study. Again, while trusting parents assume that a learning of the basics is underway in American classrooms, just the opposite is the case. This was the subject of Charlotte Thompson Iserbyt's 1999 text, the deliberate dumbing down of America (small lettering as on book cover)

Her book erased the notion that this education brand of lesser knowing is a recent "new age" type of curriculum. Ms. Iserbyt quotes from a 1933 published piece entitled, A New Definition of the Educated Man, by a Dr. (professor) George Hartman, in part; …it is the prime business of education to remake our institutions and our traditions…we must cease training people for what they are going to do and point out instead what they should do." Could the good doctor be plagiarizing a bit of Marx?

The following year, 1934 Carnegie Corporation forked out $340, 000 for the publication of a book entitled, Investigation of the Social Studies in the Schools. On a personal note, my father once asked me what my Social Studies book was about? I responded that it was my History book to which he replied, "why isn't it called History?" His question made sense then but now, I fully understand the reasoning and what that change signaled.

So, back to our need for traditional learning and with a special emphasis upon Civics. When parents demand a return to such, then our populace will, in time, understand and call for an accounting. At that time, this judiciary's abidance to its limited constitutional authority will be a demand. The absence of this is why 'the Ninth' prefers to and does roam without a leash.

This wider latitude of usurpation is common when freedom's guardians, we the people, fail their individual duty of knowing and then voicing their own sovereign authority. America's education, when excluding the traditional studies of our Founding and glorious history is not education but rather an intentional implanting of ignorance!

This mental atmosphere is dangerous and counter productive as it encourages our enemies while it belittles our Country's Constitutional relevance. The bottom line, as this Ninth Circuit reveals, is the hypothetical of when the American people don't know their rights, they don't have any rights! So, this "dumbing down' will continue until?

Our American Tragedy

January 9, 2019

Just how is it that a newly elected Congresswoman feels the need to blurt out "Impeach the motherf-----?" Just how does this square with JFK's "Ask not what your country can do for you" standard? In just fifty-nine short years, this comparative example reveals the degree of our American tragedy.

This stunner of a statement is a product from this intentional detour from former standards of education which instilled each generation with the vigor of American pride, individual decency, morality and proper citizenship. Consequently, in today's world, these four categories have largely become ignored, even to the point of incurring laughter and ridicule.

Most perplexing is this two-year display of bitterness against a duly elected President. This has continued despite our economic turnaround and low unemployment numbers. Certainly, this revisit of a citizen interrupting his private affairs so he may volunteer service to his country has indeed brought a validation of our Forefather's original design while undressing the stagnation of the modern-day career politician.

Those previously mentioned educational standards received a severe injury when a few atheist voices from seventy years past objected to prayer in the classroom. The result was an improper judicial rendering which sought to please the few dissenters but also set precedence for today's standards for personal interpretation and re-authoring of our Forefather's explicit words.

Recently, a congressional proposal from last year has surfaced because two Muslim women have been elected. This change affects a 180 year plus regulation stating that members of Congress are to enter the chamber without any headwear. Now, with the advent of these two newly elected Congresswomen, common sense must question their qualifications in light of this hatless regulation. How, in good faith to their beliefs could they accept such conformity and if not, their intent was answered not only by those we elect but by those electing committees who qualify candidates.

The point is just how does a society maintain its standards and guiding principles when conforming to its few objecting voices? What justifies the rewrite of set standards for the few? This was the case back when school prayer was deemed to be a tool for establishing an "official state religion."

Shying away from these two religious based questions, there is little doubt that time not only heals wounds but also distorts originality. Today's educational emphasis is just that, a distortion since we are now being advised that "What good is it if you graduate…and you don't know how to work in a team?"

That quip was just aired in the local paper and was authored by a department head of a University. This may offer a glimpse into just how derailed are our educational goals. As those previous quotes offer, this comparison from the traditional "three Rs" for learning the intricacies of being a team player seems to be equally rooted in this tragedy aimed at our young.

Today, we have an unhealthy dependence upon technology rather than relying upon individual's abilities. Consider that younger cashiers often seem lost when simply making change from the cash drawer. Also, what need is there for learning the cursive skills of yesteryear when texting abounds, and signatures often require one's finger doing the signature?

All this may seem old-fashioned and antiquated but self sufficiency, rather than tech dependency, should be an asset worthy of learning. Isn't a well-rounded education still the mission? There is little doubt that this decay hides behind many faces but the educational tidbits which surface all point to an intentional disorder which borders upon educational treason.

When figuring in the decline of American morality, given that college dorms are now co-ed, "hooking up" is a convenience without commitment! This is not the preferable lesson to learn, however, it dovetails with the irresponsibility of legalizing former illegal drugs.

Given this wide-open atmosphere, George Washington's Rules for Civility or his book of Quotations will never be in "kindle" form! After all, what does "Civility" have to do with anything today, especially when its replacement, Saul Alinsky's Rule for Radicals, forecasts our pending American tragedy!

The Shredding of America's Heritage

March 21, 2019

America beats strongest when her Founding Era is respected and protected. So it is that our journey forward is best with the acceptance of such a proud resume. Younger hearts must pump up the patriotism and loyalty for which our American heritage deserves. The vitality and vigor of each succeeding generation deeds their responsibility for maintaining our American values of freedom and individual opportunity for all who seek her shores.

My effort lacks any animus but rather stems from an urgent desire to publicly air what otherwise would go unnoticed. In this instance, to raise proper concerns about history's devaluing, which was recently in full view in our local paper. Lately, mainstream media outlets have discounted or revised contents to fit their narrative, typically from the slanted versions of AP releases. To that, we can now add the art of censorship when truth is in the offering.

After successive years of having my queries published in this local paper concerning George Washington's birthday omission from its daily 'Today's Birthdays' column, my latest critique fell short.

Then after roughly a week and in a fairly lengthy article regarding Betsy Ross' family bible, this publication dared to question her renown with "she is said to have sewn the nation's first flag," which was again repeated later in the piece! This article also questioned whether George Washington and Robert Morris "are said to have met with her to ask her to make the flag."

All these details point to what has, through past omissions, become a clear effort to rewrite or erase America's glorious Founding period, which sadly dovetails with the current curriculums found in our nation's classrooms.

This is systematic to what has seeped into our American perspective.

It seems that our current mindset is vulnerable to all input since we lack any foundational beliefs, whether it be historical or spiritual. It might behoove us to examine, with emphasis, all such disloyalties since our heritage pivots upon our understanding and respect.

Their decision not to publish also illustrates what they fear the most; public exposure to the truth since the truth tends to stimulate by exciting one's curiosity.

While I center this response upon one incident, this is far from being the exemption, but rather the rule. Today, we face the reality that for too long, we have relaxed while this socialist ideology flourishes. So, with congressional districts being flooded with like minded socialists, thus assuring the continuation of this anti-American representation, our time for standing and defending has indeed come.

Our heritage is uniquely singular; one which sprung from the heartbeat of freedom. Our Founders didn't wait to respond against evil; their actions were proactive in that they envisioned their increasing servitude. Never before was this the cause for such a decisive and bold crusade; one which faced such immeasurable odds. However, their belief sustained the hardships at Valley Forge and brought forth their Christmas daring over a river named Delaware.

This was their action as opposed to our present state which showcases a most formidable national weakness, complacency. This recent censoring tactic is not and should not be available or permitted in this "land of the free." Such a proud and famed heritage that has been passed down demands our renewed American pride and loyal defense. If this is too heavy a lift, then this current loud mouthed socialist craze will not only continue to censor but smother the patriotic breath which our American hearts so naturally and dearly seek!

The Natural Order of Things

July 11, 2019

Who attempts running before taking their first steps? Obviously, the order is to walk, then run. As I watch historical landmarks being desecrated and, in some cases, removed to forgotten corners, I reminisce back to my parental experiences of teaching my children the basics. There is and history will validate that there always exists an order and to it, is our best foundation.

So it is that in addressing this present-day assault against America, one must fathom out just what is so and what is not since it seems that these emotional outbursts against our Founding are of an intentional design to first degrade and then abolish our Founding and our America in general.

In 1776, a free America was declared. This first step of declaration preceded our sacrifice to actually gain that which was declared. Again, first things first. So, when dealing with these current episodes of destruction and mayhem, there is a need to review our prior disrespect and abandoning of this natural order.

Our declaration and years of struggle and sacrifice for the gaining of our independence began, what for some, is a detestable history. In large part, this notion pivots upon the dreadful issue of slavery; of which we as free Americans inherited from the British. Once America gained her freedom, a necessary order of priorities set the standard for its eventual abolition but given how infused this system was, the natural order was to first unite as a nation. This is the crux of the matter which conveniently is never addressed.

After gaining independence, we set out to govern under the Articles of Confederation, which gave way to our present-day Constitution. It was at the time of our Constitution's adoption when the subject of slavery was debated but soon it was realized that the order of things had to first establish our Constitutional government. This could only be had by a unifying vote from the original States.

In order for this to take place, slavery was the one debate which could dampen if not cripple America's beginning. So, grudgingly, it was realized that while sentiment was present for abolition, it would have to be postponed so that our country could be united first. Again, it's the order of things since without the opportunity offered by a free Country, any possibility for abolition would be impossible!

Today, that order of things is askew! The 'why' of it all is very obvious and at the same time, very frightening. It's all about the takedown of America, along with her freedoms and opportunities. Simply put, this is an in-house revolt which is using our system and its freedoms, most notably our freedom of speech and right to assemble, in order to build public dissention; this with special emphasis upon the idealistic crowd who are conveniently grouped on our campuses.

Also, today's economics has been the tool for reversing modern day parenting into this new governmentally sponsored 'day care' system. Thus, childcare began taking place outside the family unit, with differing sets of principles which might not have been family friendly. The point is the natural order of parental care was transferred onto the shoulders of paid strangers. Who can say what caused all these recent school shootings but certainly the disappearance of parenting could be a player.

Dare we say that this is not the order of things? Parents sacrifice so that their children benefit the most. Sacrifice is the normal and accepted role of parenting and once was a responsibility gladly welcomed. Hints of this unnatural change surfaced when replacing mom's cooking with the school cafeteria dishes. And what ever happened to "brown bag" school lunches?

Then there is the elephant in the room, public education. It's hard not to recall earlier times when basic learning was also a family task. The first 'public schools' were church oriented, with parental input! And when grading the product of our Founders versus today, the natural order of those days produced success, prosperity and a norm of productive citizens.

When fast forwarding to current beliefs, those who are so sure of what they don't know seem enlightened to the degree that trashing Civil War monuments and painting over a Washington mural seem overdue. Try as they might, not all change comes from man. There will be a returning to the natural order of things, and this will come from the one who is the overall Creator of all our order. Everything comes to he who waits. Again, this is just the natural order of things!

Incrementally Yours

August 22, 2019

It's the old frog in the boiling water trick. Slowly upping the water temperature permits the frog to die a happy but surprising death. This is the designed trickery behind our system of gradual increases, and it has become rampantly successful throughout America's last one hundred years.

Still vivid from my early working days was the introductory level of a wage tax assessed to all who worked within a mid-sized city's borders. Few complained about a yearly ten-dollar tax which would benefit the immediate community. This was an expenditure which didn't even register.

However, once enacted, this good intentioned charge represented the "nose of the camel." As with all taxes, that ten-dollar charge morphed into a fairly sizable percentage of one's gross income. This has become an all too familiar scenario which exemplifies the authority's continual abuse of public trust, all intended to be accomplished at an incremental and unnoticeable pace.

Another example of this insidious snail methodology for change comes with the issue of secondhand smoke. This hot button issue began with its good intentioned restrictions concerning air travel. Today, those initial accommodations, within the confines of commercial airliners has, through a growing but methodical list of restrictions, affected all public gatherings regardless of whether it be enclosed or open aired. Today's anti-smoking history is a wrap up from the successful results which incrementalism has produced.

One comparison available from this slow revamping of America's smoking habits reveals the inner workings of a "democracy," which is the liberty restricting system that too many generations have been taught exists in America. Essentially, "democracy" is a numbers game, in which once the majority has been attained, the minority lacks a viable platform and begins to suffer.

Think back to that initial anti-smoking salvo centering solely on-air travel. It was immediately accepted based upon its confined area. At the time, many more Americans were smokers. Thus, the initial target of protest centered upon the more obvious, the indefensible and at the same time seemingly understandable yet still inconsequential based upon the small numbers affected.

It became accepted that the back of the plane was a sensible trade-off. Later, it was agreed upon, although with some hesitance, that two-hour smokeless flights were reasonable. What followed was the final destination of a completely smokeless air travel industry, those long international jaunts.

This brief review, taken from two vastly unrelated issues, both with incremental parallel growth, provides proof of how societal and governmental change accomplish their mission impossibles.

When tracing the history of targeted areas, one gets the feel that the growth in numbers substantiated each restrictive step. Along the way, while non-smoker's rights grew to be recognized and protected, a strange occurrence took place which reversed who would be oppressed.

By scanning this number growth and this majority transfer, one can almost date when the oppressed became the oppressor. Airplanes and restaurants were now historical footnotes. Now, onto the open air where even the shrubbery would benefit from additional clean breathing.

This emphasis upon numbers also uncovers the most basic and fearful tenet of a "democracy." Majority rules. As such, individual rights are non-existent when faced with superior numbers. It was this inescapable fact which united our Forefather's intense disfavor of a "democracy" structured government. It was long understood that majorities often connect with and are driven by emotions and public emotions can be available for any opportunity or any opportunist.

Do not be misled by this emotional secondary smoke furor. Its flames have been stoked often by the loudest and the most influential. But, even with the "expertise" pedigree, the evils of emotions often carried the fight.

Consider that the World Health Organization produced a report that in no uncertain terms denounced the fears that secondary smoke could cause lung cancer. While this WHO report was pulled almost immediately, copies were had.

Today, little matters as to the validity of the issue and it strikingly parallels the public's belief in America being a "democracy." The strength of and duration of this misinformation lies in the emotional aspect of being right.

Another arena for gradualism is our judicial process. For quite a while, Supreme Court decisions, not to mention the decisions from the lower District Courts, have revised, misinterpreted or added onto our "law of the land." Today, this judicial no man's land allows for legal rulings which bear little to our origin intent of Constitutional law. In fact, there currently exists a growing sentiment that international tenets should be considered and/or included into our jurisprudence product.

Landmark decisions, which conflict with our basic Constitutional dictates abound and have exponentially increased as we further our legal distance from our Constitution's originalism. Its incremental flavor is such that current findings now outweigh our Constitution and have somehow become the grist for decision making; as each decision compounds into past precedence, our judicial foundation crumbles further.

Innocuous references and/or statements may also signal the commencement of the next incremental effort. Such could have been the recent offering as Obama reflected upon this recent Florida tragedy. To quote, "I think all of us have to do some soul searching to figure out how this happened, and that means we examine the laws."

Obama has exhibited little reverence for our Constitution and its limited governmental structure. The State of Florida has received much publicity over its recognition of our Second Amendment rights. Obama's mentioning of "the laws" seems irrespective to what took place. "The law" was not at fault.

Isn't it time for this creeping incrementalism, along with its companion of democracy to be given its just dues? This word, democracy, is absent in every Founding document and certainly in our law of the land, the Constitution. Its Father, James Madison voiced his objections to our being a possible "democracy" when defending the Constitutional convention's 1787 outcome by saying,

> "Hence it is that such democracies have ever been spectacles of turbulence and contentions; have ever been found incompatible with personal security or the rights of property; and have in general been as short in their lives as they have been violent in their deaths."

Not only from these Founding words but also from their original intent, we have traveled a great and disloyal distance. We must reverse course or continue our slow descent into a socialistic abyss. Even as Obama has stated, "I think all of us have to do some soul searching." That's a great start!

Communism Inside Our Gates

September 28, 2019

Often it has been bandied about as to how former President Kennedy would be considered a conservative given today's democrat platform. I wonder, especially after a stroll through the pages of our history.

For prefacing's sake, it is essential to understand that the core objective of the communist doctrine is world domination. Never mind with all the hoopla from our response after announcing the fall of the Soviet Union; just ask who was paying for all those submarines or for their military maintenance and such.

The sad bottom line to this masquerade is the degree in which Americans dismissed common sense when hearing what was pleasing and reassuring. So, let it be understood that communism has never wavered, especially here in America!

Returning to Kennedy (JFK), I challenge this latest example of media misdirection, that Kennedy wouldn't qualify as a democrat today, simply based upon one alarming piece of evidence—the Department of State publication 7277, released in September 1961, which shatters this illusion. As we shall see, this was hardly the work of a conservative and totally in line with today's socialist infection.

Also, there are massive amounts of Kennedy oratory which places him in stride with today's socialist (progressive) venue of the Democrats. Generally, back in JFK days, he believed that the communist threat was from 'without' never "within."

This was detailed in a November 18, 1961, speech in Los Angeles and was featured by The New York Times the following day. In that account, he said, in part, "the discordant voices of extremism are heard once again in the land. Men who were unable to face up to the danger from without are convinced that the real danger comes from within… they look suspiciously at their neighbors and their leaders…they find treason in our finest churches, in our highest courts." He summed up with, "but you and I …know that it comes from without, not from within."

Couple that position of communist protection with his previous United Nations speech on September 25, 1961. That oratory became the previously mentioned 7277 booklets, "Freedom from War: The United States Program for General And Complete Disarmament In A Peaceful World."

This Kennedy reference offers tenure while also contradicting today's broadcasts of a "new" or "sudden" socialist alternative by the dems. Not only did this long-ago President refuse to even consider the threat from 'within,' he endorsed the UN's authority over the US when authorizing the disarming of our Nation during his UN speech, which also included the elimination of our unalienable Second Amendment All this based upon the good faith and promises from those which included communist regimes.

While this media comparison of Kennedy to current democrats may seem trivial what has unfolded since 2016 is unbelievable, if only from the perspective of what was not realized. The usurpers have been uncovered! In response is the media's need for shock and awe verses truthful coverage.

All these similar anti-American policies and reactions, such as the media's blanketing of Trump fantastic pro American UN speech, stems from one poisonous tree. Only one nationally sized organization could call for the coordinated anti-war demonstrations of the sixties. Today, that has mushroomed into the complete abandonment of campus free speech. Demonstrations, both of the costly and violent types, have erupted and in certain cases, with institutional support. Again, those seeds from the sixties have burrowed deeper and definitely multiplied.

This communist infection has spread unabated until now. Think back to all the previous administrations which never even mentioned the word socialist or pointed out the falsity of our news industry? And all the while, that poison spread since the threat of its accountability, ala McCarthy, was no longer.

America is being sold down the river and it took a courageous nonpolitician to tell this truth. They are here and the impressionable young are their targets. Whether they are called liberals, progressives, socialists or communists, they are anti-Americans and they will destroy everything in their way to world domination.

America's Christian Heritage

February 18, 2020

May the following put to rest the false claim by President #44 that America is not a Christian Nation. Such a statement defiled the office while embarrassing the American people in general. It was so out of order that it seems directed not to we older Americans but to the younger and more gullible American students.

Such an attempt at misdirection dovetails with this ongoing effort at realigning our national course. Still, it requires an unknowing ear, which the abandoning of certain basic educational studies such as the Bible, American History and civics accomplishes. Simply put, if one isn't aware of his or her rights, for all intent and purposes, they do not exist!

So, this is a dusting off those forgotten pages of America's Founding so that our people may finally learn of our proud Christian heritage and in doing so, lay bare the tactics of these anti-American influence peddlers.

From William J. Federer's text entitled, America God and Country, we learn of a younger George Washington, in 1752, and with his own writing, created a personal prayer book containing excerpts such as, "Almighty God and most merciful Father…receive O Lord, my morning sacrifice which I now offer up to Thee." This entry preceded the evening's entry of, "O most Glorious God in Jesus Christ my merciful and loving Father…" while closing with, "I humbly implore Thee to hear, accept and answer for the sake of Thy Dear Son, Jesus Christ our Lord. Amen."

These are the reverent words from the "father of our Country." On the eve of our declaring independence from Great Britain, July 2, 1776, his General Order, in part, to his troops included, "The general hopes and trusts that every officer and man, will endeavor so to live, and act, as becomes a Christian Soldier." Finally, at the top of the Washington Monument are the words, "Laus Deo," which means, "Praise be to God."

America's second President, John Adams, wrote on 21 June 21, 1776, in part, "Religion and Morality alone, which can establish the principles upon which Freedom can securely stand." Later, on June 2, 1778, he advised,

> "In vain are Schools, Academies, and Universities
> instituted, if loose Principles and licentious habits are
> impressed upon Children in their earliest years..."

(the capitalization was his)

His son, John Quincy Adams, our sixth President stated on July 4, 1821, that,

> "The highest glory of the American Revolution was this;
> it connected in one indissoluble bond the principles of
> civil government with the principles of Christianity."

Another Forefather, Noah Webster known as the "the Schoolmaster of America" produced the first American dictionary which included a profuse amount of word definitions taken from Biblical Scriptures which resonates with his high regard that; "Education is useless without the Bible." Also, he noted in his History of the United States work that, in part, "...the genuine source of correct republican principles is the Bible..."

Also, from that published work, in part, "the religion which has introduced civil liberty is the religion of Christ and His apostles... This is the genuine Christianity, and to this we owe our free Constitutions of Government." Most applicable is his advice stating that, "All the miseries and evils which men suffer...proceed from their despising or neglecting the precepts contained in the Bible."

This sampling would not be complete without the input of Thomas Jefferson who believed that religion is "Deemed in other countries incompatible with good government and yet proved by our experience to be its best support."

From a November 4, 1820, Jefferson letter;
    "I hold the precepts of Jesus as delivered by Himself, to
    be the most pure, benevolent and sublime which have
    ever been preached to man."

Our Nation's founding and subsequent history are filled with such stated beliefs so although these are few, it validates America's Christian foundations. From any platform of authority or influence, up to and including the pulpit and judicial renderings, such facts have withered under this progressive and mindless anti-Christian onslaught. In defense, a perfect one-two punch would center on renewing our Blessed Christmas season, followed by ridding our holiday list of the nondescript "President's Day" and returning Washington and Lincoln's individual days for their due honor.

An Anniversary Still Without Answers

May 3, 2020

The April 18, 2020, issue of the Daytona News Journal featured an anniversary article entitled,"25 years after Oklahoma City bombing, anxiety remains high." Although presenting just a rehash of what supposedly happened, it never-the-less renewed my curiosity and interest of a past event which was hastily concluded with a seemingly hasty trial, guilty verdict and death sentence.

Immediately eye catching was its opening line, the falsehood which from that day in 1995 has been taken almost as gospel, "In the 25 years since a truck bomb ripped through a federal building…" This glosses over the debilitating effect of an explosion concerning the distance between the truck and the Murrah Building.

Consider the long-ago analysis which William F. Jasper reported from an interview in the August 7, 1995, issue of The New American magazine with General Benton Partin, the Air Force's top demolition expert.

Briefly, when viewing the damaged remnants of the Murrah Building, the General stated, "yes, this was a big bomb with a big blast. But most people fail to appreciate how ineffective a blast is in air and how dramatically its destructive potential drops off just a few feet from the explosion." Also, more incriminating was his view that "The total incompatibility with a single truck bomb lies in the fact that either some of the columns collapsed that should not have collapsed or some of the columns are still standing that should have collapsed and did not."

On October 27, 2002 the Philadelphia Inquirer did a similar anniversary rerun (seventh) with a more lengthy article by staff writer Ken Dilanian in which he wrote, of the late Senator Specter, "Specter sat in his office listening to a former television reporter" (Jayna Davis) "who alleges that contrary to the findings of the largest federal investigation in history, the 1995 Oklahoma City bombing was orchestrated by a secret terrorist cell of former Iraqi soldiers working for either Saddam Hussein or Islamic extremists, or both."

Later, Dilanian adds that "Accompanying Davis in Specter's office were a former CIA agent and a former defense intelligence officer, BOTH OF WHOM ENDORSE HER THEORY." (My emphasis) Also, Dilanian wrote of former CIA director James Woolsey who "was quoted as saying that the nation would owe Davis a debt of gratitude."

This 2002 article entitled, "7 years after Okla. Bombing, whiff of conspiracy lingers," served to minimize or trash an event, in which the "FBI reviewed 30,000 witness statements and one billion documents," and by linking to an assassinated President. Quoting former FBI deputy director Weldon Kennedy, "It's just like the Kennedy assassination. These conspiracy theories are going to go on long after you and I are gone."

Well, given that lengthy Journal article, which continued the pattern of ignoring any possibility of a foreign conspiracy, it seems that its slant was perfect timing in that it dissuades any further curiosity. Today, all that is remembered is that McVeigh was the American responsible for the bombing. Yet, further reading of that 2002 article refers to questions that still remain unanswered and, more importantly, are forgotten. I'll illustrate.

Jayna Davis covered the bombing for Oklahoma City's KFOR-TV says, "she has 2,000 pages of evidence which present a persuasive argument that 4/19 was a precursor to 9/11."

Dilanian continues with, "Seven weeks after the attack, Davis broadcast a report identifying John Doe 2 as an Iraqi refugee who had been working as a laborer In Oklahoma City. She gathered sworn affidavits from seven people who say they saw this man – who has a tattoo on is left arm and bears an uncanny resemblance to the John Doe 2 sketch – with McVeigh."

This information was not based upon a single unidentified source, but from seven people who all saw this foreigner. As Mr. Dilanian further writes, "The report noted that, shortly after the bombing, the FBI put out an all-points bulletin seeking a late-model brown pickup truck and indicating that two Middle Eastern men were believed to be in the truck. She says witnesses later placed the truck at the Iraqi man's place of employment, where he WORKED WITH OTHER FORMER IRAQI SOLDIERS." (Again, my capitalizing)

Eighteen years later, the acceptance that America gave to that seemingly tireless and uncorrupted FBI investigation which encompassed "30,000 witness statements and one billion documents" has been severely tarnished by it's more recent and supposedly exhaustive investigation of the Trump Administration, which produced its falsified impeachment circus and then more recently, revelations concerning Gen. Flynn's railroading. The 1995 Oklahoma City dead end investigation may suggest that what is current may well have been employed at least twenty-five years ago.

The purpose of mentioning these recent FBI capers is simply to present a pattern that defies the available evidence in one case while later attempting to prosecute based upon the unfounded and false. Clearly, there is a misdirection being formulated and pursued by governmental authorities.

In conclusion, I return to Mr. William Jasper's investigative reporting in a later issue, April 20, 1998, of that same publication. The title of Jasper's piece, Proof of Bombs and Cover-up, says it all while again casting a dim view upon the FBI's creditability and investigative results.

No less than the "renowned physicist Samuel Cohen, the inventor of the 'neutron bomb'" stated, "I believe that the demolition charges in the building placed inside at certain key concrete columns did the primary damage to the Murrah Federal Building." This he said back in June 1995! He also concluded that, "It would have been absolutely impossible and against the laws of nature for a truck full of fertilizer and fuel oil – no matter how much was used – to bring the building down."

Can one believe that Dr. Cohen's statements were actually lost in those one billion documents or 30,000 witness statements? It would be asinine to suggest that the doctor's beliefs were not then available "to the largest federal investigation in history." I might add, just as asinine as was that recent FBI driven impeachment fiasco!

It's Now Stand-up Time

June 13, 2020

The current acts of banditry—such as looting, shooting, torching and overall destruction —have all been sadly eclipsed by the submissive non-actions of the Seattle Mayor who surrendered a section of the city to ruthless terrorists. Conversely, it's now time to take a stand —that is, if America is still worthy of protecting!

I remember way back when Vietnam was still an issue of debate; one caller to a Philly talk program stated something like; I'll take up arms and fight when the Viet Cong come sailing up the Delaware! Well bucko, their identity has changed but their intent is still the same domination that communism always marches towards!

Today's mightier version of those sixties protests has deserted the campus for the entire American landscape. All this from pictures of a man being gruesomely murdered by an outlaw policeman and his uniformed cohorts. Indeed, our heartfelt response of protest, which no one will dispute, was a valid reaction. However, its validity has become secondary as other horizons beckon.

That calling is an echo from the sixties when America's youth aided and abetted her communist enemy! What's noticeable is that of all the news, interviews and endless chatter from our inept media pundits, the one possible agitator or identity that is never uttered is that "C" word, Communism! As with most printed news of the day, what is not mentioned is usually more relevant.

Even General George Patton believed that step one is to identify the enemy and equally important, to study his tactics. However, a more relevant quoting comes from none other than Saul Alinsky's Rule for Radicals, "Pick the target, freeze it, personalize it, and polarize it." Alinsky considered this so important that he added, "The other important point in choosing of a target is that it must be a personification, not something general or abstract."

Citing Alinsky is obviously relevant since it's his tactics that are on display today. His "personification" requisite was answered as the rioters transformed that single criminal act of murder onto America's weak link of past racial discriminations, intolerance and yes, slavery. While the crime of murder is inherently personal, this historical recall ignites a broader appeal.

And yes, Alinsky's tactics are classic to communism and remain alive from the sixties when a proper protest for an impersonal declaration of war was ignored. Instead, noisy street chants were deeply personal with its "personification" from a fear of being drafted. This was the rule until the Lottery system; after which levels of protest immediately receded.

With both the sixties and today's replays, our young and gullible were and are targeted for their inexperience and easy acceptance but more so for the down the road and lasting effects of the adage, "as the twig is bent, so grows the mighty oak!"

How is it that our need to identify our enemy still awaits? Since 2016, this simmering revolution has been brewing. As each attempt at negating the 2016 Presidential results withered on the media's vine, the desperation and the stakes grew substantially.

Recently, those staked targeted America's economy, her work force and associated livelihoods as all were deemed an expendable trade-off that would be justified from a swift Trump exit. Once that price level became acceptable, what are a few lives, businesses or even cities? These are the calloused tactics of the communist motto: the end justifies the means.

Do not believe me? Don't, but consider the written words of the former communist defector Whittaker Chambers, from his best selling tell all entitled, Witness on Page 9, in part, "Communists are bound together by no secret oath" but by "a simple conviction: It is necessary to change the world."

Philosophy aside, more pertinent with today is his; "For the revolution is never stronger than the failure of civilization. Communism is never stronger than the failure of other faiths." (Page 193)

The graphic imaging of Floyd being murdered ignited protest, which was understandable and bi-racial in content. With the media's saturating coverage, protests engulfed America. Floyd's murderer was charged and arrested yet the intensity of protest quickly degenerated into rioting, looting, and which included the murdering of approximately a dozen police officers.

Over the last few days and nights and with many stores empty, this rioting mob has leveled their mischief upon long ago established Civil War statues. Now, anger attacks and destroys without any possible connection to Mr. Floyd while the authorities do little. Such acts are the deeds which together result in what Mr. Chambers wrote, "the failure of civilization."

Since this destructive spree against Confederate monuments has a history long before Mr. Floyd, the victimization of our civilization must be considered as the actual target, now with its traction being enhanced by the sorrow of a nation.

America must have leadership that is willing to identify this threat and that maintaining order isn't an option. If we turn our back, close our eyes and ears, Seattle's partial submission will represent only a beachhead for the future. As Chambers wrote, "A Communist breaks because he must choose at last between irreconcilable opposites – God or Man, Soul or Mind, Freedom or Communism." (Page 16) His decision should be taken as a prelude to ours.

Biden

America Needs Enemy Identification

March 23, 2021

Are we so preoccupied 24/7 that we remain oblivious to the basic needs and responsibilities which freedom and our country requires? If so, just what happened to all our time that was saved by these modern gadgets and conveniences? Or could it be that we've been subliminally encouraged that such useful cautions were only appropriate years ago?

To be honest, a major roadblock to the public's interest or even its curious nature is the various blackout methods employed by all media sources. In any case, this public attitude cannot continue without incurring a dangerous and uncertain future.

As the list of anti-American forces increases in parallel to our public's submissive nature, a main cog driving this new brand of mental warfare continues to enjoy anonymity throughout many decades. So as this progression of disorder and destruction proceeds without any accounting, identifying its cause and its source becomes critical.

The reality of this whodunit is that it flies the socialist/communist banner, and it has long before those tumultuous sixties. Unknowingly, this effort has been orchestrated by the rarely mentioned consortium of the Council on Foreign Relations, or simply, CFR!

Its tentacles of influence and control are everywhere but especially within our nation's military, our media, public education and government. Its influence has brought to our nation's military many reductions, revisions and regroupings; all designed to conform to civilian PC levels, of which are antithetical to the basic mission of the military.

America's winning military—that is before the CFR's heightened infiltration—was based upon the highest possible levels of training, moral and winning results. Today's merging with civilian standards is embarrassing and disastrous since the military's workplace of physically exacting and lethal demands have undergone civilian grooming.

The late Admiral Chester Ward, who was a CFR member for nearly two decades, explained the CFR's purpose as: "submergence of the U.S. sovereignty and national independence into an all-powerful one-world government." Pertinent of what President Trump endured was Ward's 1975 remark, "In the entire CFR lexicon, there is no term of revulsion carrying a meaning so deep as 'America First,'" Wow, this 1975 utterance provides proper relevance to the media's later day Trump drubbing!

On the one hand, we had this ongoing slide to a more socialistic global community versus Trump's return to the more traditional America First platform. Today, every step taken is to ensure that such a political hiccup will never be repeated, so it stands to reason that all CFR hands will be at full alert with their media and governmental brethren.

During the Trump years, his task was constantly challenged by these in place elitists. According to the CFR's own 2018 Annual Report, 457 were in government, the media and news outlets numbered 319, and our educators topped out at 1107. Is there any wonder as to why Trump met roadblocks or even why our school's curriculums became so manipulated?

This CFR influence and control, at some point, must be realized for what it is! Obama's National Security Advisor General James L. Jones, who was not CFR connected, inadvertently admitted to its control when stating, "I take my daily orders from Dr. Kissinger, filtered down through General Brent Scowcroft and Sandy Berger" All three hold membership! The CFR's style of operating was made clear when Kissinger, who as Secretary of State under both CFR Presidents Nixon and Ford, replied when questioned about the legality of a certain policy, "The illegal we do immediately; the unconstitutional takes a little longer."

Additionally, now a former Presidential candidate Hillary Clinton, was a 2009 guest speaker at the opening of the new CFR headquarters in Washington D.C. where she boasted, in part: "I have been often to… the mother ship in New York City, but it is good to have an outpost of the Council right here down the street from the State Department." "We get a lot of advice from the Council so this will mean I won't have as far to go to be told what we should be doing and how we should think about the future."

Again, these are the people with their hidden but structured agenda to which Trump contended with daily. One can easily see why he was considered such a dire threat but more importantly, it's clear that without his defiant CFR position, this global conversion from freedom to communism would have continued with a quicker pace!

Credit the Council's success to largely its hidden existence. While conservatives, including President Trump, have hinted about it, those three letters never are spoken. Instead, we hear the usual aliases; "the establishment," "the elitists" "the power brokers," "progressives" and most recently, "the globalists" but NEVER those three little letters! Only the late Rush Limbaugh would utter "CFR," or its longer form, but only within the context of a discussion but never being the subject itself.

This year will total a century since its creation, while still being able to avoid public recognition. When connecting America's setbacks to the degree of CFR influence, its commanding foreign policy voice and subsequent global input all began in earnest following WWII, as did our pitfalls!

This call to identify is not picayune since its continued public unknowing provides a free and unhampered atmosphere which covers and protects their anti-American deeds and deceptions. Just about any inconceivable or hard to imagine outcome can be traced back to this band of anti-American plotters. Glaring is the consistency of American pit falls and it's that consistency which should now ring the bells and whistles of our self preservation instincts!

Our Educated Future

April 19, 2021

What follows is a forecast which few will enjoy and less will agree with. Having previously referenced John Dewey as "the father of American progressive education," what remains hidden from the public is who or what supported his anti-American educational crusade? Money was essential and as the saying goes, it provided the root of his evil agenda! Without this financing his socialist dream would remain just that!

Dewey's original seed money came from none other than John D., as in Rockefeller! Actually, his Foundation was joined financially by other similar tax-exempt foundations. Successful and wealthy industrialists backed Dewey's anti-American scheme simply for the reasoning that the late Samuel Bloomfeld and Alex Newman's Crimes of the Educators explains, "To Dewey, the greatest obstacle to socialism was the private mind that seeks knowledge in order to exercise its own private judgment and intellectual authority."

From that same text we learn Dewey believed that "the traditional curriculum of the primary school had to be radically changed…to remake American education as an instrument to bring about socialism." So, thanks go to those exempt foundations for financing what became today's socialist mentality!

America's educational system is now in the toilet and has been headed that way for many generations! Suffice to say that America's future has been uprooted. She cannot exist with such broad-based ignorance, coupled with this lack of appreciation or respect, let alone without any expectation of maintaining our usual pride and patriotism. Obviously, this adversely affects our national security, so education or its lack is indeed a possible "act of war."

Over time, our educational journey from family "log cabin" instruction to a local church-based venues, and now finally to this broad-based unconstitutional authority known as the Department of Education has follow exactly its own creative script so why such shock or denial?

Left to its own devises, without limits, expectations and certainly without any formal accounting, today's educational product has depreciated from the traditional subjects provided in those local venues to this college/university initiation where our children's instructors have been groomed by socialist minded misfits who are strictly anti-American and pro-collectivist in their thought and student input.

Still, without alarm bells ringing, loving parents send their children off to school with the long-ago memories and expectations of their own learning experiences. For whatever the reasons, few attend if still being held, parent/teacher nights. This disassociation had previously been accepted during the infant years when day care centers were the answer for dual-income families.

Clearly, not only have we lost our educational direction and purpose, but there is also a concerted effort to divert basic learning so that the result will produce a needy, dependant worker who will be easily controlled simply by his own inabilities. This possibility is not even on the discussion table because of its self-incriminating reality but that doesn't make it go away or not be true! Without action, this sad state of unknown will eventually become a total jungle like atmosphere which even these socialist planners have yet to envision. However, in the meantime, there are profits to be made.

Somehow, this subject needs to surface into our conscience state. Sooner or later, it will and if it waits too long, its effects and results will be deadly! Hell, already it's being previewed as emotions rule decision making, as has been the case with this George Floyd excuse for anarchy in the streets!

While the procrastinator will delay, America's educational duty needs a General Patton like person to break this silence and command a plan of action. It better happen soon since in the future, there will not exist such a capable individual!

With Foreign Hearts and Minds

May 16, 2021

Just as our communist enemy assigns their tactics onto their adversary, what they offer misdirects. Therefore, the proper perspective is skepticism. Without any thought or question, we are slowly being globalized and revolutionized. Therefore, a decision awaits; what do we, as a people, hold dear and what options best address our vulnerability?

One clear result from this globalized/communist freak show is this attempt at eliminating our national borders. This crisis, from an issue that was previously under control, points to foreign motives by those we have elected who also and sadly possess foreign hearts and minds. Cold hearts are the mainstay of communists.

This and other anti-American initiatives merely reflect a continuation of past American disloyalties which include siding with and/or aiding the communist cause in China, Hungary and Vietnam. Also, Washington's officially adoration included saluting Castro as "the George Washington of Cuba!" This clearly presents a picture of misguided if not foreign loyalties.

Point being, it's not only more of the same pro commie agenda, but now, with the democrat's blanket of control over Congress, the White House and subverting our Supreme Court into a globalized rubber stamp, their appetite for brash policies along with a Constitutional brazenness has become routine.

Such a routine is sadly on display with this Critical Race Theory nonsense. Not only are this saturating America's classrooms, but it is also now a guide within our corporations, which was recently reported by The Epoch Times' piece, "Disney Embraces Race Politics, Critical Race Theory In Employee Training." Also too, our military is undergoing this CRT transformation!

We prideful Americans must become the legendary "squeaky wheel," a bee in the socialist bonnet! We can no longer remain silent and passive! Now is the time to rally around our most formidable weapon, the truth! Wishing and hoping won't do it! And violence is not an alternative, just the opposite!

We need to work in a peaceful and legal manner. We need to irritate them by using methods unique to Americans. This can be accomplished through the promotion of our strengths: a unified front speechifying time honored truths, outward displays and proclamation of our faith, flying our American flag, and all other irritating historical flags and banners, a willing self sacrifice for the homeschooling of our young, and a boycott of any corporation which defies our American ideals! These are but a few of our effective tools.

All this in tandem by safeguarding our own precious minds from their tactics of group identification, corralling Americans by certain identifiable pig pens—such as male chauvinist, gender abuse, feminist, gay bashing, Christian right winger and of course the most recent, white privilege, of which presented many with an invitation from Uncle Sam of a two-year paid "vacation!"

These mindless charges work best when students remain incapable of individual thought or judgment. One of those buffoons, either Stalin or Lenin, commented something about not being about to make a socialist out of an individualist. Apparently, judging by our public indoctrination of the young, this concern has been addressed.

My foreign hearts-and-minds reference is a two-edge sword. Yes, those we elect are not the most trustworthy of the American spirit, yet it is those who vote who are also swayed by anti-American motives; one such being this "something for nothing" dependency! Our push back begins with the individual, with 'we the people.'

There is a reason why our past, both good and bad, is being desecrated. America's heritage is indeed glorious to the point that with a working knowledge of such, socialism must flounder if not remain irrelevant. Our Forefathers, while not perfect, were far sighted, self sacrificing, loyal and honest with visions which continue to be applicable today.

The father of our Country, George Washington advised;

"The name of AMERICAN, which belongs to you, in your national capacity, must always exalt the just pride of Patriotism, more than any appellation derived from local discriminations."

This one remark shatters any thought to their lacking relevance with modern day concerns. Especially when such concerns involve the removal of our Freedoms and Unalienable Rights from God!

The Emptiness of Democrats

June 1, 2021

Hillary Clinton has set the proper tone for this latest writing when she told CNN that, "You cannot be civil with a political party that wants to destroy everything you stand for…" From that perspective the democrat's emptiness with this current leaderless Presidency screams out for a redressing.

The end result from hijacking a Presidential election without a positive platform, worthwhile policies or any hope for capable leadership is that it should merely be a "fluff" in a windstorm. However, this reality, as disgraceful as it may be, is mere trimmings of a more sinister design.

The common link of these empty suits is that they lack any American loyalty! This is even harder to swallow when coming on the heels of one who placed America First! Consequently, these sighs and moans of remorse are now the yearnings for that gruff but pro-American leader's return.

The term "emptiness" is perfectly suited since the modus operandi of the Democratic Party is nothing if not for hypocrisy and falsehoods. It matters little that both venues are antithetical to freedom and liberty since these, along with capitalism, are their most despised targets. Such anti-American conduct has also aided in the production and encroachment of those with foreign hearts and minds!

All sorts of negatives are born from such an empty administration. First to emerge is this disappearing act concerning accountability. This lack of any accounting induced last year's city after city destruction without any responsible enforcement. Laws without applicable muscle are useless so the continuation of this rioting only tweaks the socialist as they labor for America's downfall.

Democrat policies are firmly based upon the unfeasible, impractical and of course the hypocritical. Think about it. Which party supports abortion yet is against capital punishment? How about the normality of requiring an ID when buying beer versus the democrat's howling against such when casting a ballot? This stance against voter ID defines their intent for enhancing voter corruption.

The most ludicrous of stances is this male invasion of female sports based upon gender equality. Democrats support this "trans" domination of first place trophies while swearing that women are equal to men, even in the military's more strenuous and possibly lethal branch of combat arms! Obviously, in both cases and contrary to their feminist position, their hypocrisy is jeopardizing female self worth, achievement and even safety!

What hypocrisy can't deliver lying often does! This tactic comes from the Marxist handbook stating, "The end justifies the means." One tenet of Marxism denounces all religious faith so therefore, Americans were told an outlandish lie, by none other than President Obama; that America wasn't a Christian nation. Forget the massive amounts of documentation to the contrary, Obama said it and as Goebbels (Hitler's propaganda chieftain) believed, tell a lie often enough and eventual it becomes the truth!

Blatantly insulting is the lying when Biden Administration lackeys state that our southern border is closed and secure. This despite footage of thousands continuously running into our Country illegally! Viewing this film sickens as does the knowing that just about the entire democrat effort is a falsehood aimed at achieving the sinister goal of America's destruction! Gone are the days when both parties were pro-American. Today, one of America's two major parties, along with snippets of the other, are made of anti-American/pro-socialist ideologues!

This situation needs immediate redressing. The most direct cure would be the elimination of democrats at all levels of governing. And it won't be any big loss since their party is an empty suit!

God's Precious Gift

December 5, 2021

Today in church, I witnessed God's gift, the most precious gift of love between a husband and wife. During the service, there sat a couple, of near if not of retirement age—nevertheless, a husband and wife of many years.

During a scripture reading by the pastor, the lady reached over with a loving smile and just touched her husband. The look on her face was indeed priceless. The husband's stoic appearance managed to turn toward her and nod affectionately. This communicative exchange between the two is the gift of an enduring love that has been Blessed, especially when being in the House of The Lord.

Over the years, this expression of love and happy togetherness has been seen during religious services often. Being in the presence of our Lord often binds the commitment and devotion to each other even stronger. This is the precious gift which ensures a happy and worthwhile union.

Sitting there, I was moved by this simple act since I was without the one I love due to an uncontrollable circumstance. However, as I watched this particular husband and wife, I was both rich from the love in my life and yes, lonely for her and her affectionate touch and smile.

Life offers no guarantees. We all are here for a short time so when love arrives, grab hold, commit, protect and cherish for there will be a day. This I offer to all my married friends who by their daily lives, often argue over what, in the end, is really not even important. Often it just comes down to "being right."

I remember my parents and their spats over nothing. They loved each other just as deeply as today's couple but having the last word or being right got in the way temporarily. But then again, we all know about the making up!

We can't spend all our time in church, in an atmosphere which brings out the truest of feelings and closest of times, so if possible, later that day or during the week, when the next time a disagreement arises, step back and think about what really matters. I certainly wish I could do so with my lady.

Fundamentals of Freedom

February 7, 2022

The cornerstone of America's independence was with our Forefathers' belief that each unrelated statute from the British, when taken in total, spelled the eventual subjugation of our people. As the late writer and author William Norman Grigg quoted, in part, "they chose to go to war against the mightiest empire on earth over what were, at the time, potential abuses."

This was America's rightful and determined beginning. Since then, what the heck happened? Who today would sacrifice all based upon a possible peril? I suspect that few know of or would agree with James Madison's insistence that every citizen should "take alarm at the first experiment upon our liberties." With time's passing and education's redirection, this tidbit has been trashed! Obviously, his expectation that Americans would treat their freedoms with what he termed "prudent jealousy" was another victim.

James Madison recalled that

> "The freemen of America did not wait till usurped power had strengthened itself by exercise, and entangled the question in precedents... They saw all the consequences in the principle, and they avoided the consequences by denying the principle."

However, the perceptions of the Forefathers necessitated the public's belief and support if resistance was to be attempted. As Mr. Griggs relates, "But it was their success in educating the public at large about that conspiracy and mobilizing a critical mass of the colonial population to defeat it, that led to American independence."

As stated, the most critical need for gaining freedom was, as Mr. Griggs states, "educating the public." Thus, today's education has eliminated any studying of our Forefathers, their reasons, beliefs, and efforts, much less their eventual crafting of our Constitution. Alarmingly, this is an elementary need when striving to subvert America into a communist state.

Even prior to the war for independence, in 1774, Samuel Adams remarked,

> "the depravity of mankind, that ambition and lust for power above the law are...predominant passions in the breasts of most men." Then there is Patrick Henry providing his concern that "I dread the depravity of human nature...I will never depend on so slender a protection as the possibility of being represented by virtuous men."

Within all our beings is our element of human nature, which composes both good and bad inclinations. This ever-present influence is the reasoning for our Constitution's designation of govern- mental "don'ts," which today has spurred the detractor's reference of it being "a negative charter." This is hard to debate but so is the fact that our Constitution remains effective, and the reason why it remains so relevant is simply from its curtailing of man's (women) common frailties.

The most knowledgeable of our Founders' original intent was a Supreme Court jurist, the late Antonin Scalia. From a book entitled Scalia Speaks, which is a collection of selected Scalia speeches, the judge stated, "The Court is partly to blame for law students' failure to study legal history and traditions." Having avoided such schools for higher learning, I still understand that "law school" curriculums solely emphasis the "case law" of the Supreme Court rather than "the law of the land," our Constitution.

Also, consider this lengthy Scalia perspective, "But perhaps the Court's most destructive line of decisions relating to civic education is the line of decisions involving the Religion Clauses. As I have mentioned, the Founders' believed morality was essential to the well-being of the republic, and that religion was the best way to foster morality. Religious values were therefore central to the Founder's aspirations for civic education."

As Scalia's words convey, education in the days of the Founders was both for the student's learning and for the building of a moral and proper American citizen. This educational venue was due to the above-noted Samuel Adams quote. That 1774 quote of Adams certainly conveys both a more accurate depiction and reasoning of today's events than what is offered daily on CNN or MSNBC!

Seriously, this reading should be by those who have the most years to come, those who have children to raise and rear, and a country waiting to be saved. Your time is approaching, in sync with today's emerging crop of citizen volunteers. America's surest remedy is to follow our Founders' time-tested and proven beliefs! With God's help, this will be the path chosen.

What's Right is Right

May 24, 2022

America's newscasters, a vocation which now only holds prestige in the minds of those highly paid and polished spin doctors, are waiting for Florida to interject its annual hurricane disasters since there is only so much murder and mayhem that the daily "news" audience can withstand.

Also, we should still question how our 'family entertainment' went from "who-dune-it" mysteries, westerns and Perry Mason episodes to this constant suffocating of news alerts?

But now, onto the grimier state of our union. At what point can the smirks disappear when broadcasting the latest insult to America's former society of sustained law and order? I mean when will the proper authorities get off their duffs, open their eyes and ears to the latest wrongs against our people?

All societal sectors are currently undergoing a transition led by this new age set; you know those who somehow "know better" before their introduction into being a productive citizen. And authoritative at such an early age! What's really amazing is that those who have been productive, experienced life and enjoyed success are actually listening and even implementing these illogical theories.

Also critical to America and her future are those who hold positions of authority yet refuse to act accordingly. Much has been bandied about the billionaire Soros and how he has financially supported his brand of communist ilk into such high-ranking law and order positions.

Apparently, this is a credible claim which also awaits addressing, but by who? DeSantis needs imitating nationwide!

Also, our reliance upon not only morality and decency but just plain 'ole' common sense has become victimized. How can our college educated teachers undertake a mission which introduces so much gender nonsense and misery into the minds of our youngest? And while parents are properly reacting in a most vigorous manner, again, where is America's structured authority? How did this degenerated thought become classroom appropriate?

I am sorry but there is more to correct than just new age thinking, although that in itself is now a hefty task. We have a system that has been incrementally infested by the industriousness of a termite; in the dark and never stopping its erosion by munching away our educational tenets.

During the lifetime of my generation, which spans well over three quarters of a century, much has been discarded. Growing up around our WWII heroes, we then watched as both the Korean and Vietnam Wars were undertaken without the legal sanctioning of a Congressional Declaration.

In the latter instance, I often wondered as to the organized protest effort of simply "Hell No, I Won't Go" while never bringing up such an addressable and firm legal point! In retrospect, seems as though the planting of those anti-war divisions within our society were the more pressing aspect on the road for building today's anti-American unrest.

History and common sense agree that America's darkest days were resolved by our Civil War. This high cost for correcting a sinful wrong was probably the only avenue for its correction at the time. Today, in our post segregation era, which ended another intolerable wrong, we are or were well onto unifying all our people; that is until the cancer of communism sprung onto the democrat platform.

What needs addressing, in a most calm and mature manner, is the reality that America is under a domestically groomed assault from the decades of college graduates who have been lectured into embracing these Marxist doctrines. The destruction of all that is of historical value, along with this attempted decimation of the American family and our faith in God sadly validates this clear communist corruption of the American mind and spirit.

We can either stick our heads in the sand or become the pro-American authorities for which today's America so sorely lacks. Similar to those "school board moms," we, each in our own peaceful way, need to stand in defense of America the Beautiful. If we remain passive, not wanting to offend while agreeing that up can be down or there is no right versus wrong, then we are not what we have claimed and were so privileged to inherit at birth; the title of being an American!

What's Right is Right II

June 6, 2022

Time is critical to fix America so familiarizing ourselves with our Forefather's proven tenets would greatly aid in our reduplicating the efficiency of their limited and successful form of governing.

Formally, America's governing included the input from "public servants" who interrupted their private affairs for the betterment of our Country. Consequently, those Americans of the day were more involved, informed and eager to maintain and protect their Blessings.

However, America's modern success and growth also included the formation of political parties which at first influenced then became dictatorial over our national direction. This despite the Farewell Address of then President Washington when, in part, he warned of; "...the danger of Parties...the baneful effects of the Spirit of Party...This spirit, unfortunately, is inseperable from our nature..." (Spelled as quoted)

Our reliance upon common sense informs us that what is discounted, ignored or denied to our young is simply due to its truth-based value. In order to institute a revamping of America, it was deemed such advice should not be assessable. Throughout my lengthy life, this has been the rule so that today's children are not even familiar with America's Pledge of Allegiance.

What Washington warned of is now "everyday" normal and is sadly exemplified by today's heated controversy of this pending reversal of Roe v. Wade. This blasphemous decision has divided Americans, as seen by the opposing forces of pro life and pro choice. This intense division is such that each of our fifty States are now colored by either a

Republican red or a Democrat blue marker. Again, Washington's words are echoing.

A side note: such turmoil is the surface action from the former undercurrent of these anti-American socialist/communist ideologues who have risen to the surface from fear of a Trump rerun. Since his election ambush, their expediency for taking America further away from her Constitutional foundation and Christian doctrines has greatly intensified!

In addition, this growing Spirit of Party captured our governmental watchdog known as America's "free press." Accepted under the moniker of a "liberal press," it's conversion from truth to falsehood is now a powerful public information arm spewing democrat philosophies but was finally outed by its well deserved "fake news" labeling. This, from an outspoken American rarity; a nonpolitical "people first" President.

Also, slow is the changing of our personal conversations; including our identity of being an "American," which now has become hyphenated when attaching Italian, Irish, German, or African American to our being. Then came the highlighting of these un-American catchwords or causes; most notably with the three Ds of Discrimination, Diversity and Democracy. At the same time, fallen from public favor were the three Cs of Christianity, Constitutionality and Capitalism. Again, all influenced by the supremacy of one party and aided by its abiding news outlets

That "D" word of Democracy is scary when judging its endurance against its truthful nemesis of a Republic, especially when reciting our Pledge of Allegiance; "…and to the Republic for which it stands…" This sadly indicates the growth of our public ignorance over our Country's actual structure of governing; again, the power of Party over Country.

Another example of this Spirit of Party was bellowed when democrat officials condemned parades associated with our patriotic July Fourth celebrations and our military celebrations on Memorial Day and Veterans Day. Such occasions were denounced for being events which would bolster the ranks of the Republican Party.

Finally, and appropriately, Washington's words sum up today's serious misgivings and dangers. In defense of our Constitutional principles, he warned:

"All obstructions to the execution of the Laws, all combinations and Associations, under whatever plausible character...are destructive of this fundamental principle... However combination or Associations...may now and then answer popular ends, they are likely, in the course of time and things, to become potent engines, by which cunning, ambitious and unprincipled men will be enabled to subvert the Power of the People"

Certainly, prophetic words of advice, which along with Washington's name, are being erased from public awareness but when voiced and realized, adds muscle to his warning against "the baneful effects of the Spirit of Party!"

Just Who Are the Clowns

June 27, 2022

Such a question rates our attention. Our American affairs are in the tank which explains why this identifying task is so numerically overwhelming. Given that these Bozo contenders are many, so are their misdeeds.

Back during the Ebola epidemic, how many of us remember our American military being deployed by Obama, thousands, to aid with the enforcement of medical martial law on the Ivory Coast? The military is supposedly for America's defense, not for foreign humanitarian purposes!

Also concerning is our current Bozo in chief shutting down a plant which totaled over 40% of America's baby formula production, all due to an unsubstantiated plant contamination claim!

Also, clown Biden then enacted the power grabbing and unconstitutional Defense Production Act, DPA, which, as writer Steve Byas relates, "sets the precedent for the president to step in and control American businesses." Somehow, his prioritizing of baby formula was based upon a 1950 defense act enacted for addressing "a potentially dire national emergency, such as warding off invasion by a foreign power." (Byas quote)

I mention both instances of what Americans are not informed about versus what falsehoods that these media-based talk shows propagate on a daily basis, such as Trump is not "Presidential" or "Jan6 was an insurrection!"

I realize that for some, such news blips are boring but how about another tidbit that slipped through the watchful eyes of our so-called free press? It so happens that this un-Presidential President refused to issue this DPA abusive power grab when mobilizing the production of ventilators during that Chinese virus scare. Instead, he wrote an Executive Order in defiance of Pelosi's insistence for employing the DPA's questionable authority.

The most obvious of clown shows is under the United Nation's tent. Such a three ringer is to be expected from when their predecessors who drew up the UN's original charter. It was anti-American from the start since America's chief representative was none other than that communist clown Alger Hiss.

Suffice to say that overall, it's mission for ensuring world peace still awaits! Yet somehow, its inept authority has mushroomed into other sectors.

Still, with clowns being clowns, past dud performances matter little when another performance is scheduled. Given its inept and corrupt record, its continued existence, beefed up by its global adherence to its authority which only encourages more of the same! Such is now the case with the UN's World Health Organization. (WHO)

Joining forces, writer Alex Newman explains that "the UN World Health Organization (WHO) and the Biden administration are plotting an unprecedented power grab to build a planetary biomedical police state. Think Shanghai during lockdown, but worldwide." This is not conspiracy thinking since Biden's DPA usage documents his hunger for power.

Also, what gives this scenario merit is its public blackout. Similar to the blackout of Trump's Presidential un-DPA conduct, what is not mentioned are the inconvenient facts of the story. Given the enormity of WHO's future, when ignoring such possibilities, "fake news" needs to add "accomplice" to its "fake" logo.

With each passing day, "accomplice" is a better fit. Consider the supposed two remaining 'conservative "news" outlets: Fox News and News Max. How is this in such a progressively dominated information industry? Simple, they are permitted with certain conditions which managed to insert the progressive's intent. An obvious point is their slam dunk drubbing that America is a "democracy!" Even to the point that political commentator Dick Morris' own show is so falsely titled!

Then there's the hallowed radio time slot of Rush's (Limbaugh) show which is now showcases by two clowns who couldn't empty Rush's trashcan let alone replace his hard hitting, effective and accurate commentary. They are embarrassingly trivia based on practically every broadcast!

The American people, who believe in America's Founding, are being treated to this three-ring show. Clowns dominate because unlike the traditional version, they are not easily identified. What is needed is the old American traditions of skepticism, doubt and curiosity; with such useful assets, assessing the UN's universal lack should result in its long overdue relocation overseas, and without our membership! It's a real three ring circus!

From Whence Our Beginnings

July 3, 2022

On our two hundredth and forty sixth year of giving thanks and celebration of America's declared and Blessed Independence, I prefer evaluation of these unsettling times to whence we were a more pious and grateful people.

During this vast expanse of time, much has been replaced and improved as America's parade of innovations has revolutionized more than just our industrial base but life in general. Little doubt exists as to the huge benefits which have improved our living and our Country. However, there is always a cost in life and America's transformative cycle is no exception.

Most deeply affecting, as witnessed by today's social turmoil is the weekend violence occurring largely in our urban centers; those which Thomas Jefferson predicted would become as corrupt as Europe's when America's reached similar density proportions.

Today's living continues at a very high expense, both in lives, property and societal needs. As such, this menagerie requires our attention so as to determine the reasons for today's violence and social discord. The intensity of unrest is such that our search is best served through a comparative view of when times were of a more peaceful, orderly and thus respectful exchange.

Obvious is the loss of quiet moments of personal thought, and a freedom to worship with a reliance upon a Higher Being. I mention this simply based upon a universal acceptance and reliance upon His supportive presence to both community and government. Today, His replacement is violence, immorality and the spontaneous taking of life. The bottom line is that America cannot continue down this road!

To realize the total irreligious genre of young America, excerpts from that era should jolt, which just might be what the doctor ordered! If the following is too "whatever," I'm sorry but your time will not be wasted. Hopefully, such morsels will strengthen and redirect to what needs addressing. So, the following are a few unknown revelations from a work entitled, America's God and Country by William J. Federer; detailing an America based upon standards which have long since been trashed. Basically, it's from a time when America accepted and rejoiced with her Christian based living.

Back in 1831, it was reported that a judge in Chester County N.Y. refused to admit the evidence of a man who declared he did not believe in God on the grounds that the witness had destroyed beforehand all the confidence of the court in his testimony. The New York Spectator reported the judge as saying, "that he knew of no cause in a Christian country, where a witness had been permitted to testify without such belief." Can you imagine this judgment today? This took place in our 55th year of Blessed independence.

The opener of New Jersey's Constitution of 1844 stated, "We, the people of the State of New Jersey, grateful to Almighty God for the civil and religious liberty which He hath so long permitted us to enjoy and looking to Him for a Blessing upon our endeavors to secure and transmit the same unimpaired to succeeding generations, do ordain and establish this Constitution." This was in our 68th year of our Blessed independence.

A main pillar of public education in America, McGuffey's Reader, debuted in 1830's and remained instrumental till 1920's. In the Forward of McGuffey's Reader, Our Christian Heritage, he wrote,

> "The Christian religion is the religion of our country. From it are derived our prevalent notions of the character of God, the great moral governor of the universe. On its doctrines are founded the peculiarities of our free institutions."

This text originated in our 60th year of Blessed Independence. Such religious learning was not banned from the classroom but was then considered normal and expected.

America's journey has been hijacked by the lures of monetary possessions, instant gratifications and baseless emotions from mostly a whimsical should be' reasoning. Right and wrong has vanished for it requires an inherent responsibility along with a concurrence to societal order. Today's secular lure has given way to the deepest of depravities which communism thrives upon.

Clearly this historical recall tells of a time when human frailties were tamed and tempered by religious beliefs. That is the difference since these urges are consistent with our human make-up but were controlled through our love and fear of God, wishing "y'all" a happy and reverent Independence Day.

Enough is Enough

October 10, 2022

I am confused by this lack of curiosity. It's most glaring when the questionable continues without pause or notice and becomes adopted into the mainstream of society. One such instance is this compulsive adaptation to this hand texting mode of communicating. Talking is still natural, quicker, easier and offers more personal contact since the inflection of the voice response also carries meaning.

An offshoot of communicating trend seems to have leaped into the democrat's handbook. As Biden so incoherently demonstrates, there is little need for any verbal contact with one's constituency since the vote now may be based upon both party support and drop boxing, which leaves the individual in a political limbo!

Given this indifference from personal contact, as former phone conversations and now older campaigning styles require, many have become desensitized into accepting this reclusive style of campaigning. Insultingly, these "do nothing" candidates now expect your vote without first telling you, in person "Why!"

In addition to this distancing, for some time, unknown quarters of influence have hand picked their obedient candidates, which essentially turns the primary selections into a side show and with our citizens remaining in limbo.

Recalling past years, the skids were greased for an unknown "peanut farmer;" and then later, in the case of Obama, after giving just one reportedly 'inspiring' convention speech. Somehow, after this one presentation, his brief Senate exposure became secondary as he was quickly anointed the dream candidate of the dems. The general election became a slam dunk as the media pumped up Obama as possibly being "the first black President" along with being "the Messiah." However, it was a time when candidates still communicated verbally.

Fast forward to the "do or die" tactics of 2020, after gleefully taunting Trump to run in 2016, those "insiders" recovered from their 2016 shock to both grease and buy the skids on election "day" of 2020. However, their candidate was of such disarray that campaign speechifying had to be limited to just debating events which were minutely controlled. This absent tactic could actually evolve into the democrat campaign play book!

Also prominent with this disappearing act is the fact that democrats lack any positive policies, which may make the absent candidate a permanent act. How can they debate or campaign promise after scorching the Constitution's limitations for the sake of their reckless policies? At this point, given their inability to offer a positive or a Constitutional agenda, my previously stated confusion centers upon how a certain segment of voters can remain so blind and stubborn when endorsing this outlaw brand of so-called leadership?

Appropriate to the adage "birds of a feather flock together," Biden's "win" has opened the flood gates to a vast array of undesirables and incompetents who also refuse to communicate verbally. The democrat's Senate selection from Pennsylvania provides the perfect example. He is running a solitary and silent campaign bid without a policy platform or even an accepted past employment record! Fetterman is typical of this emerging new Democrat breed who expects to win without providing any reason for your support!

Once our standards become this debased, those in the darker quarters of the political game can only smile since all that is required is to garner up public emotion for their next empty suit. Essentially, the democrat party just needs a body, a name to register. Biden has proven that! Also, the Republican response, which is passive at best, provides their silent encouragement. This mild form of complicity provides a bipartisan blanket of "see no evil" non-action which, in turn, is why "things never seem to change."

Campaigns have always been verbal affairs which usually occur in the "public square." Yet these types of contests may now be reminiscent of the dinosaurs. They represent the last vestige of civic participation for renewing our governing structure within a Constitutional Republic. In accordance with the democrat's urgency, they now appear as a relic, a past nuisance which conflicts with today's new candidate brand. Such a non-product requires a loud shout of "enough is enough" from all of America's voting public!

From The Ground Up

October 18, 2022

In his Farewell Address of 1796, President George Washington summed it up the best. Referencing political parties, he stated, "the baneful effects of the Spirit of Party...This Spirit, unfortunately, is inseparable from our nature..." (Washington's capitalization and spelling) Even at that early time, Washington recognized the problem and directed his concern towards our human inclination for aligning with and creating political parties.

This slice of Washington's wisdom defines what feeds and perpetuates today's ailing government. Also, this may have been the reasoning behind our Founder's belief that the most worthwhile and efficient government would be from the ranks of its involved and knowledgeable citizens sacrificing their time and effort for the country's betterment.

Apparently, Washington anticipated what has come to dominate our government and its selected elected. No longer is the government comprised by such volunteers, given today's handsome salaries. And office holders are now groomed through academia's political science corridors.

This deterioration of individual quality and purpose has been replaced by the party's criteria, hinging upon one's potential adherence to its political platform and goals. Hence, this answers why "nothing ever changes!"

Hopefully, the state of our nation has awakened the people to realize the need and value that our Founders realized with citizen involvement. Although today's possibility of a direct military threat has lessened, a differing ruination has evolved which has spurred an "if not now, when" type of volunteerism. Instead of military service, as was with WWII, Americans are now interrupting their often-successful careers so that they may help save our country from this present-day destructive agenda.

In addition to this public awakening, we in our own way can aid this turn around with a self appraisal of our own seemingly minor derelictions of duty, a duty which all Americans, along with their Blessings of freedom inherit at birth. Simple acts such as turning a blind eye to what is not right, being too busy to take time out for one's community or simply to voice an objection in a letter. This may seem picky but in total, it mounts up and contributes to a weakening of our liberties and is relished by the opportunists who gain from such apathy. An active and informed populace automatically strengthens our United States.

Many are these "turn the other cheek" instances may seem trivial; however, they send the wrong signals. And we, when judged by our human instincts, are all guilty. Too many detrimental sayings or ideas have seeped into our inner beliefs and subsequent actions. One such is, "you can't fight city hall." We have all heard this and might even come to agree with.

On a larger and more affecting scale, my writing often rags on about America not being a democracy and yes, such monotony may seem endless, but these socialist falsehoods are publicly aired on the same repetitive daily scale. However, in America's defense, more Americans are denouncing this media dribble.

We who value our Country must be supportive in every manner. Those who have initiated this present disunity, criminal violence and societal discord fear both our involvement and our knowing minds. Consequently, those that question is labeled in order to dispel any inquisitive interest or individual thought from catching on.

These instances are just a sampling of what our daily routines take for granted. However, nothing is trivial when defending against these subversives. America has awakened and at a time in which little time is left to alter her present direction. What needs changing are the few becoming the many who will thankfully shoulder the responsibility which freedom demands. Washington cautioned about human nature always needing to be strengthened. "Going with the flow." will sway if left unattended.

Determining the worth and impact of these current citizen volunteers is by judging the actions of their opposition. Need I say more? All that is heard from the dems is their hating of our "America First" beliefs! What else to expect from a party which has embraced socialism?

America is Blessed by her legacy of freedom and by those who take pride when being called an "American." Let us swell their numbers by making America the hill that we make our stand on. Our time is now!

Our Forefather's Design

November 1, 2022

This call to peaceful and legal action hopefully centers our attention upon what really is our threat, an ongoing and classic communist revolution! America and her people are dangerously close to losing their freedom, not only just to vote in the 2024 elections but a total loss! If these commies continue unabated, 2024 could be just another calendar year marking this creeping public control.

Forget the PC acceptable "liberal," "progressive," "far left" or "globalist" designations. This is America's crunch time, so we need to grapple in the dirt, as did our forefathers. This threat isn't going away and with every graduating class, their numbers grow from intense indoctrinations.

Their BS is there for all to recognize. These midterms have enlisted the most overrated "orator" in America's political history; Obama with his sad attempts to motivate through fear and slander. His slick words only spout with emotional fits of false charges which heighten public anger and resentment with all the wrong reasoning. He only instills and further incites the hatred which has been mainstream since Trump's 2016 shocker against this globalist ruse. Again, globalism is just a word mask for hiding its corporate partner of communism!

Americans are a most generous and humanitarianly aware people, but they are also the most trusting and when misguided, their trust can be reversed to work against them. Just as our freedoms afford the widest of latitudes for all, including our enemies, so it is with our good-natured trusting, as with, "that can't happen here" refrain. Well, it can, and it is!

Next week is our Country's "fourth quarter with no time outs!" Forget 2024 or the media's hogwash about a DeSantis versus Trump showdown. That's their dream, not ours. If 2024 is still a happening, Trump will do just fine, and our great Florida Governor will be his greatest fan. This is just another scheme to cloud the picture and to rid Florida of DeSantis leadership.

The midterms are our ticket, and the communists are most fearful of America's potential from true public servants who have volunteered for service to their Country. They are without the chains of either party's control. They are proven individuals from a variety of vocations. Most importantly, they profess true allegiance to our Constitutional Republic and are supportive of another Make America Great Again Presidency!

These communists have been so forceful and arrogant that they have rid themselves of any meaningful midterm messaging. Think about it; not only feeding the youngest of illegals to this pedophilia sickness, but these open borders are also providing a gateway for their lethal drugs without a caring thought to the thousands of Americans dying as a result. How about their halt of America's energy independence to such a degree that our diesel fuel supplies are now limited to just twenty-five days! Also, this Biden regime allocated millions of barrels of oil from our Strategic Supplies to Red China! That's right, it's RED China, not just China!

Then there's the communist interpretation of a woman's right to privacy which supposedly permits an abortion minutes prior to birth! Or how about Biden's diddling around young girls and his adamant support for gender reconstruction from decisions made by grade school children? Next our youngest could be buying beer and tobacco products. Also, there is the murder of an unarmed lady, who was a thirteen-year Air Force veteran, by a police officer who was exonerated of any wrongdoing!

These actions or policies are not American but are typical of the communist heavy booted style of authority. So be a democrat or continue to hate Trump if that pleases but realize why family members around the Thanksgiving Day table are being so quiet. It's from the mistrust of their family members and for being so uncomfortable with those they love but who have become so damn Anti-American!

It's not political any longer. It's now about freedom and survival! Our Founder's design for citizen involvement has reappeared as the most feared aspect of the midterms. Our enemy knows better than we that this could mean. Their effort is towards the betterment of our Country, not the betterment of their damn political or communist party!

REFERENCES

1. The U.S. Constitution
2. George Washington, A Collection, edited by W. B. Allen
3. The Bullet Proof George Washington, by David Barton
4. The History of the American Revolution I, II, by David Ramsey MD,
5. Friends of the Constitution, Writing of the "Other" Federalists, 1787-1788
    Edited by Colleen A. Sheehan, Gary L. McDowell
6. View of the Constitution, St. George Tucker, 1752-1827
7. The Federalist Papers, Edited by Clinton Rossiter
8. The Anti-Federalist Papers, Edited by Ralph Ketchum
9. Common Sense, Thomas Paine
10. America's God and Country, William J. Federer
11. Military Journal of the American Revolution, 1775-1783 by James Thacher, MD
12. American Dictionary of The English Language, Noah Webster, 1828
13. McGuffey's Reader, 1836, William H. McGuffey

ABOUT THE AUTHOR

Jim Bowman is a seventy-eight-year-old retired boilermaker, who was raised in and around the Philadelphia area, who briefly attended college, and who is an Army veteran of Vietnam. He is the proud father of daughter Kimberly and son Gregory and is also the grandfather of Connor, Emma, and Aidan. He is a self-taught writer with over thirty years of experience, which includes having published This Roar of Ours.

His love of golf offsets each frustrating round of which only he earned. He has resided in Ormond Beach, Florida, for over twenty years but still misses those Philly cheesesteaks and hoagies!

www.ingramcontent.com/pod-product-compliance
Lightning Source LLC
Chambersburg PA
CBHW051136120626
46547CB00012B/824